The Economic Theory of Annuities

The Economic Theory
of Annuities

Eytan Sheshinski

PRINCETON UNIVERSITY PRESS
PRINCETON AND OXFORD

To Ruthi
who makes lifelong planning worthwhile

An Annuity is a very serious business; it comes over and over every year and there is no getting rid of it.
—Jane Austen, *Sense and Sensibility*, chapter 2 (1811).

Contents

Preface

THIS BOOK IS AN analysis of the functioning of private annuity markets. On the demand side, individuals who face uncertainty about their longevity want to insure their lifetime consumption without leaving unintended bequests. On the supply side, insurance firms are able to provide predetermined payouts to annuitants by pooling uncorrelated individual risks. Equilibrium prices and quantities of annuities depend crucially upon the ability of insurers to identify and price differentially purchasers of annuities with different characteristics. The focus is on two issues: *asymmetric information* about differences in individuals' survival prospects and other pertinent variables, and the *ages* at which these differences unfold. These questions are at the heart of resolving the "annuity puzzle": Contrary to theoretical predictions, the market for private annuities is extremely thin, particularly the demand by individuals in their early working years.

The book starts with a general treatment of survival functions, applications of stochastic dominance concepts, and a characterization of changes in longevity. The demand for annuities is derived from a model of individuals who jointly choose their lifetime consumption and retirement age. The effects of imperfect annuitization options and changes in longevity on individuals' behavior and welfare is discussed extensively. We highlight the interaction between insurance and labor markets, a subject that has not been adequately discussed in the literature.

Subsequent chapters analyze *pooling* and *separating* equilibria in order of increasing complexity. A novel application is the possibility of *bundling* insurance products in order to reduce the *adverse selection* present in stand-alone markets. Applying statistical population theory, we analyze (chapter 12) the macroeconomic effects of annuitization on aggregate savings and growth. A number of empirical studies attribute the surge in savings and growth in Asian and other countries to increased longevity of the populations of these countries. This chapter sheds light on the debate whether this surge is transitory or permanent.

Interest in private annuity markets grew as reform proposals for public social security systems called for the creation of funded, privately managed personal accounts to finance retirement benefits. Indeed, my decision to write this book grew out of a graduate course in public economics that I taught at the Hebrew University and Princeton University. It is a theory course on market failures, covering issues of externalities, public goods, natural monopolies, and second-best corrective taxation. Building on the pioneering work of Diamond and Mirrlees (1971) and the vast literature that followed (as viewed from the early book by Atkinson and Stiglitz (1980) to the recent books by Myles (1995) and Salanie (2000, 2003)), welfare costs are measured in terms of deviations from full-information, efficient, competitive equilibria. As social security reform became a top policy issue, I devoted an increasing part of the course to subjects such as a comparison of the effects of pay-as-you-go and funded systems on individuals' retirement and savings decisions. This topic introduced two new elements into the course. First, the rationale for government involvement was postulated to be the shortsightedness of individuals, which came to be called *bounded rationality*. I was aware, of course, that once individuals' cognitive limitations are introduced in one form or another (a number of *behavioral* models are now available), this may have implications on other core issues of public economics beyond long-term savings. I thought, however, that this exploration should be postponed until we have a more general behavioral paradigm with proven relevance in varied circumstances.

Second, continuing to assume individual rationality, I thought that government intervention in providing social insurance (retirement benefits, disability and healthcare insurance) may be justified because, inherently, insurance market equilibria are not Pareto optimum. In particular, I was looking for a general model that analyzes separating and pooling equilibria in private annuity markets. Such an analysis would enable a concrete examination of whether and how the government can improve upon the competitive allocation. Not finding a comprehensive treatment of annuities, I decided to write lecture notes, which later evolved into this book. So, while this book is pure theory, the motivation came from public economics.

The modelling in this book is quite general, for example, time (age) is treated as a continuous variable, and functions are generic. This generality produces simpler and more intuitive equilibrium conditions and comparative statics compared to the two- or three-period models customary in the literature. The level of mathematics used should be no problem to graduate students in economics or finance.

I faced major decisions about what *not* to include in the book, and I would like to point out three omissions. First, I do not address the question of the proper investment policy for insurance firms aimed at covering their annuity obligations. Matching of investments and obligations (and the related question of the proper measurement of risks) is an important issue (see, for example, the succinct recent discussion by Merton (2006)), but our focus is on the demand side and I thought that this subject deserves separate treatment. Second, the reader will not find a discussion about the proper mix of public social security systems and private annuity holdings. There is a vast literature on this subject (see, for example, the World Bank view in *Averting the Old Age Crisis* (1994)). It raises institutional and distributional issues that, I felt, could not be given adequate consideration in a book on theory whose major goal is to examine the functioning of private insurance markets. Third, I was contemplating whether to include a chapter on behavioral aspects of the demand for annuities. Many experimental and empirical studies indicate that these factors play an important role in this market. While occasionally I discuss suboptimal behavior by individuals (e.g., chapter 6), I decided, in the absence of a sufficiently general model, not to include a separate chapter on this subject. I plan to address behavioral issues in subsequent research.

Almost all the chapters in this book contain original material not published previously, and the last chapter (16) presents a suggestion for a new financial instrument, *annuity options*. I have had some encouraging discussions on the implementation of this idea with people who run pension funds. It is very much in the spirit of the agenda put forward by Robert Shiller in *The New Financial Order* (2003): There is a vast potential for expanding and innovating new insurance instruments.

Completion of a book like this presents an opportunity to recognize intellectual debts. I studied at MIT during the "golden age" of the 1960s. The "explosive exuberance" of the lectures by Paul Samuelson, Robert Solow, and their colleagues, and the discussions (sometimes night-long) with my classmates, have had a durable imprint on my work.

Modern theory of risk and insurance markets has been framed by Kenneth Arrow, and his impact on the analysis in this book is no exception. I have benefited much from discussions with him over the years about annuities and related issues. The seminal paper on annuities by Yaari (1965) has been the benchmark for many subsequent developments, including this book. My debt to Jim Mirrlees and Peter Diamond is evident. Jointly and separately they developed the modern theory of asymmetric information and self-selection equilibria and analyzed their welfare implications.

I am particularly grateful for valuable comments on an early draft from Kenneth Arrow, Peter Diamond, Avinash Dixit, and Jerry Green.

Finally, I wish to thank Zeev Heifetz for excellent and speedy scientific typing, Avital Madeson for taking care (with good spirits) of all office and technical chores, and Seth Ditchik, of Princeton University Press, for promptly bringing this project to completion.

The Economic Theory of Annuities

CHAPTER 1

Introduction

"And All the days of Methuselah were nine hundred sixty and nine years: and he died" (Genesis 5:27).

AN ANNUITY IS A financial product that entitles the holder to a certain return per period for as long as the annuitant is alive. Annuities are typically sold to individuals by insurance firms at a price that depends on the payout stipulations and on individual characteristics, in particular, the age of the purchaser.[1]

The demand for annuities is primarily based on the desire of individuals to insure a flow of income during retirement against longevity risks. In the United States today, a 65-year-old man and woman can expect to live to age 81 and 85, respectively, and there is a substantial variation in survival probabilities prior to and after these ages. Brown et al. (2001) report that at age 65, 12 percent of men and 8 percent of women will die prior to their 70th birthday, while 17.5 percent of men and 31.4 percent of women will live to age 90 or beyond.

Figure 1.1 exhibits the trend in age-dependent survival probabilities in the United States for cohorts from 1900 to those expected in 2100.

It is seen that while the hazards to survival at very young ages have been almost eliminated, increases in survival rates after age 60 have been slower, leaving substantial uncertainty about longevity for those who reach this age.

Uncertainty about the age of death poses for individuals a difficult problem of how to allocate their lifetime resources if they have no access to insurance markets. On the one hand, if they consume conservatively, they may leave substantial *unintended bequests* that in terms of forgone consumption are too high. Annuities and life insurance can jointly solve

---

[1] Annuities can be purchased or sold. Selling an annuity (going short on an annuity) means that the individual sells an income stream conditional on the seller's survival. Holding a negative annuity is an obligation by the holder to *pay* a return per period contingent on survival. Most loans to individuals are, at least partially, backed by nonannuitized assets (collateral), but some can be regarded as negative annuities. For example, credit card debts have a high default rate upon death because these debts are not backed by specific assets. As observed by Yaari (1965) and Bernheim (1991), the purchase of a pure life insurance policy can be regarded as a sale of an annuity. We discuss life insurance (bequest motive) in chapter 11.

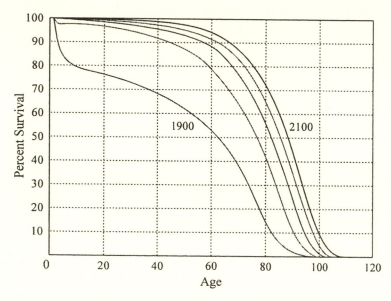

Figure 1.1. Survival functions for the social security population in the United States for selected calendar years (1900, 1950, 2000, 2050, 2100). (*Source*: F. Bell and M. Miller, *Life Tables for the United States Social Security Area, 1900–2100*, Social Security Actuarial Study No. 120, August 2005.)

this problem. A life insurance policy, by pooling many mortality ages, provides for a certain bequest whose value is independent of the age of death. Annuities, sometimes called *reverse life insurance*, also pool individual mortality risks, thereby ensuring a steady flow of consumption during life. As we shall show, access to these markets is extremely valuable to the welfare of individuals.

This stands in sharp contrast to the small private annuity markets in the United States and elsewhere. Several explanations have been offered for this *annuity puzzle*. One obvious explanation is that public social security (SS) systems, providing mandatory annuitized benefits, crowd out private markets. However, the SS system in the United States provides *replacement rates* (the ratio of retirement benefits to income prior to retirement) between 35 and 50 percent depending on income (higher rates for lower incomes). This should still leave a substantial demand for private annuities. Another potential explanation is annuity market imperfections. It was once argued that insurance firms offer annuities at higher than actuarially fair prices. This was largely refuted when annuitants' life tables, reflecting high survival probabilities, were used to calculate expected present values of benefits (Brown et al., 2001).

Davidoff, Brown, and Diamond (2005) suggest that a mismatch of the age profiles of benefits paid by annuities with individuals' consumption plans is a possible cause for partial annuitization. Bequest motives, shifting resources from annuities to life insurance or to other means for intergenerational transfers, have been offered as another explanation for the low demand for private annuities. It is difficult to rationalize, however, that this motive leads individuals to plan the drastic reductions in their standards of living implied by exclusive reliance on SS benefits (50 percent of the population in the United States has no pension beyond SS). Increasingly, *behavioral explanations*, based on *bounded rationality* (in particular, shortsightedness), are offered to explain the reluctance to purchase deferred annuities early in life.

While each of these explanations may have practical merit, we do not pursue them in this book for two major reasons. The first is methodological. Our objective is to analyze the demand for annuities by perfectly rational individuals and the functioning of competitive annuity and life insurance markets with only informational constraints. Analysis of such an idealized model economy is necessary in order to provide the background against which one can evaluate the impact of various practical constraints, behavioral or institutional, such as those outlined above. Second, many SS systems are currently being reformed to allow larger reliance on private savings accounts, which are expected to substantially increase the demand for private annuities. This lends urgency to the need to develop an understanding of the functioning of a competitive annuity market.

Among the arguments about annuity market imperfections that we do not incorporate into this analysis are those whose reason is not considered to be apparent. For example, annuity issuers seem to have no difficulty providing payout schemes that vary with age. If individuals are planning for rising or declining consumption with age, it can be expected that the market will provide annuities with a payout profile that matches these consumption plans.

On the other hand, we devote much attention in this book to the impact of *information* on the functioning of annuity markets, in particular, to the transmission of information to the issuers of annuities about changes in health and other factors that affect survival prospects.[2] As they age, individuals become better informed about future survival prospects, depending on factors such as health and occupation, and about the value of other needs and desirables, such as bequests. The

---

[2] Insurance firms that conduct medical tests on prospective clients sometimes find out information that is initially unknown to the subjects of the tests, but these subjects can soon be expected to become aware of the test results. It is interesting to speculate to what extent insurance firms have an interest in not fully informing clients, if so permitted.

uncertainties early in life create a demand by farsighted risk-averse individuals for insurance against different potential future outcomes. We analyze extensively to what extent a competitive annuity market can satisfy this demand by pooling individual risks.

When dealing with future longevity risks, market efficiency and its welfare implications depend critically on two considerations: first, whether there exist long-term annuities that yield returns as long as the holder is alive; second, whether information on each individual's survival probabilities does not remain *private information* but becomes known to annuity issuers. When this information is common knowledge, then the market for long-term annuities can provide efficient insurance against the arrival of information on survival probabilities (which we call *risk-class classification*). When the information on an individual's risk class is unknown to annuity sellers (and is not revealed by the individual's own actions), then annuities are sold at a common price to all individuals. The result is a *pooling equilibrium* that is characterized by *adverse selection*. That is, facing a common price, individuals with higher longevity purchase larger amounts of annuities, thereby driving the equilibrium price of annuities above prices based on the population's average longevity.

An issue not covered in this book is the relation between stock market risks and annuities. The issuers of private annuities, whether insurance firms, pension funds, or banks, have to choose a portfolio of assets that will best cover their annuity obligations. These assets, whether traded shares, bonds, or housing mortgages, fluctuate in value. Hence, optimum portfolio rules have to be formulated in order to reach a desirable balance between returns and risks.[3] Typically, there is a link between these optimum portfolio rules and the flow of expected revenues and outlays on account of annuities. There is an extensive financial literature that deals with this and related issues. Analysis of this link and the functioning of a competitive annuity market is complex and seems largely separate from the issues discussed here.

In developed economies, the bulk of annuities are supplied to individuals by mandatory, government-run, SS systems that provide retirement benefits. The worldwide trends of population aging and lower birthrates created serious solvency problems for these systems, which are based on a pay-as-you-go principle. Much of the research in recent years has focused on the design of SS reforms aimed at closing these deficits. The issues involved are not only the economics of annuities but also much broader issues such as the effects on aggregate savings, labor incentives,

---

[3] Unlike banks who face potential systemic risks (e.g., a "run on the bank"), annuity issuers can rely on fairly stable flows of outlays and revenues.

and distributional concerns (e.g., the effects of price or wage indexation on the level and distribution of benefits, the cross-subsidization implied by various defined benefits formulas, and the alleviation of poverty in old age), to name just a few. We think that it is best if these and other important policy issues are treated separately, confining our analysis to the more narrow but well-defined question of the functioning of a competitive annuity market. It is hoped that, this analysis can provide an underpinning for better SS reform designs.

1.1 BRIEF OUTLINE OF THE BOOK

setting the interaction among longevity, retirement age, and the savings required to maintain a steady lifetime consumption flow. Benchmark calculations show the need for significant savings toward retirement (beyond retirement benefits provided by social security) and the required response of consumption to changes in longevity or in retirement age.

Chapter 3 defines the technical concepts used throughout, in particular the definitions of survival functions and hazard rates. It also defines the precise meaning given to terms such as "more risky" or "higher longevity," using the concepts of *stochastic dominance* developed in the theory of finance. In particular, it describes the possible effects of changes in longevity on survival probabilities at different ages.

Chapter 4 lays out the basic model from which the demand for annuities is derived. Individuals who face longevity risks and have access to a perfectly competitive annuity market choose a lifetime consumption path and an age of retirement. A *no-arbitrage condition* for a competitive equilibrium is shown to equate the rate of return on annuities to the *hazard rate* (plus the interest rate on non-annuitized assets).

Having derived the demand for annuities, optimum savings, and the age of retirement, chapter 5 performs comparative statics calculations showing how these choices are affected by changes in income and by changes in longevity. The effects of a positive *subjective time preference* by individuals and positive interest rates are also analyzed. The classic Yaari (1965) result is demonstrated: When faced with longevity risks, it is optimum for individuals to annuitize all savings.

The time preferences of individuals are shown to be important in determining the dependence of optimum retirement age on longevity (a much discussed question in the design of SS reforms).

Chapter 5 also analyzes the behavior of an individual who has no access to an annuity insurance market. In the face of uninsured longevity risks, it is shown that varied attitudes toward risk preclude many of the predictions about individual responses derived in chapter 4.

In chapter 6 we analyze the implications of deviations in subjective beliefs about survival probabilities from observed market survival frequencies. Some empirical studies (e.g., Manski, 1993; Gan, Hurd, and McFadden, 2003) found only small such overall deviations, though these are more pronounced at older ages. The recent literature on quasi-hyperbolic discounting (Laibson, 1997), positing decreasing discount rates over time (age) (viewed as a problem of self-control), can be interpreted in our context as the adoption of excessively pessimistic survival prospects when deciding on optimum consumption and retirement age. This game-theoretic inconsistency conflict leads sophisticated individuals to use the purchase of annuities early in life as an instrument to steer later "selves" in a desirable direction.

Chapter 7 analyzes the potential distortions created by *moral hazard*. This occurs when individuals can invest resources (such as medical care and healthy nutrition) to raise survival probabilities. In a competitive annuity market, this leads to an inefficient resource allocation due to overinvestment in life extension. This is a well-known result in insurance markets: The cause of the inefficiency is that individuals disregard the effect of their actions on the equilibrium rate of return on annuities. Essentially, these distortions are due to *asymmetric information* because if the issuers of annuities could ascertain medical and other expenses that enhance longevity, prices could be conditioned on these expenses, thereby eliminating the distortions.

Chapter 8 tackles a particularly important issue and lays the ground for discussions in subsequent chapters: When faced with uncertainty about future survival functions early in life, to what extent can the annuity market provide the insurance desired by risk-averse individuals against alternative realizations. It is shown that this is not possible if there are available only *short-term* annuities. It is then demonstrated that when *long-term* annuities are available and the information about individuals' risk classes is common knowledge, then the competitive annuity market equilibrium is *first best*. The discussion includes a derivation of the equilibrium rate of return on annuities purchased prior to the realization of heterogeneous risk classes.

Chapter 9 analyzes the characteristics of a pooling equilibrium, where individuals' risk-class identities are unknown to annuity issuers. In particular, it is demonstrated that because of adverse selection, the pooling equilibrium price of annuities is higher than a price based on average longevity in the population.

Complementary to uncertainty about future survival probabilities, chapter 10 considers the effects of (uninsurable) uncertainty about future incomes. How does this uncertainty affect the demand for annuities early in life and the ex post chosen age(s) of retirement?

Chapter 11 incorporates a bequest motive into individuals' lifetime plans, leading to the purchase of life insurance. Particular consideration is given to *period-certain* annuities (e.g., 10-year-certain), which provide not only a flow of income during life but also payment of a lump sum to a designated beneficiary if death occurs soon after annuitization. The optimum allocation of resources between annuities and a life insurance policy is derived for a population with heterogeneous life expectancies (a continuum of risk classes). Again, the focus is on timing and asymmetric information. When individuals make decisions prior to longevity realizations, a competitive annuity and life insurance market equilibrium attains the first-best allocation. In such an equilibrium, regular annuities and life insurance dominate the holding of period-certain annuities. In contrast, a pooling equilibrium opens up the possibility for a variety of types of annuities to be sold in the market. Specifically, it is shown that in a typical pooling equilibrium individuals with high longevities hold regular annuities and life insurance, those with low longevities hold period-certain annuities and life insurance, and those with intermediate longevities hold both types of annuities and life insurance.

Through their effects on individual behavior, one can trace the macroeconomic implications of annuity markets. Chapter 12 examines the transmission to aggregate savings of changes in individual savings due to changes in longevities. The analysis incorporates the induced long-term changes in the population's age density function due to the changes in longevities. Conditions that ensure that *steady-state aggregate savings* increase with longevities are derived. The results refute some recent empirical studies predicting that the increase in aggregate savings observed in many fast-growing economies will eventually be dissipated by the dissavings of the larger fraction of old individuals.

Prices of annuities implicit in social security systems invariably imply cross-subsidization between different risk classes (e.g., males/females). What are the guiding principles for a tax/subsidy policy that improves social welfare? Chapter 13 applies the theory of optimum commodity taxation in examining the utilitarian social welfare approach to the pricing of annuities under full information. It is shown that second-best optimum pricing depends on the joint distribution of survival probabilities and incomes in the population. Specifically, a low (high) correlation between survival probabilities and incomes leads, under utilitarianism, to subsidization (taxation) of individuals with high (low) survival probabilities.

The setting for the standard theory of optimum commodity taxation (Ramsey, 1927; Diamond and Mirrlees, 1971) is a competitive equilibrium that attains efficient resource allocation. In contrast, annuity and other insurance markets with asymmetric information are characterized by non-Pareto-optimum pooling equilibria. Chapter 14 analyzes the conditions for optimum taxation in pooling equilibria. We focus on the general equilibrium effects of each tax in such equilibria and derive modified *Ramsey–Boiteux conditions*. These conditions involve the additional consideration of how individuals who purchase different amounts because of adverse selection react to a price increase resulting from a marginal tax rise.

It is well known that monopolists who sell a number of products may find it profitable to "bundle" the sale of some of these products, selling them jointly with fixed quantity weights. Bundling cannot occur in competitive equilibria when products are sold at marginal costs. This conclusion, however, has to be modified under asymmetric information. Chapter 15 demonstrates that pooling equilibria, characteristic of insurance markets, may typically have such bundling. These bundles are composed of goods whose unit costs are *negatively correlated* when sold to different risk classes, leading to a smaller variation of the bundled costs with individual attributes. This tends to reduce adverse selection and hence leads to lower prices. Annuities bundled with medical care or with life insurance are prime examples, and there is some evidence that in the United Kingdom some insurance firms link the sales of annuities and medical care.

Chapter 16 provides a general analysis of sequential annuity markets and proposes a new financial instrument. The analysis generalizes the discussion in chapter 8, allowing for uncertainty early in life about longevity and future income. It was previously shown that when uncertainty is confined to longevity, the early purchase of long-term annuities can provide perfect insurance, implying no annuity purchases later in life (and therefore no adverse selection). This is in stark contrast to evidence that most private annuities are purchased at advanced ages. It is demonstrated in this chapter that allowing for uninsurable income uncertainty leads to a sequential annuity market equilibrium with an active "residual" market for short-term annuities.

In the general case analyzed in chapter 16 the competitive annuity market equilibrium is second best. This raises the question whether there are other financial instruments that, if available, could be welfare-enhancing. We answer this question in the affirmative, proposing a new type of *refundable annuities*. These are annuities that can be refunded at a *predetermined price*. It is argued that a portfolio of such annuities with varying refund prices may enable individuals to better adjust their consumption paths to information about longevity and income that unfold over a lifetime. It is shown that these annuities are equivalent to *annuity options*, available in the United Kingdom, which allow their holders to purchase annuities at a later date at a predetermined price. Such options may be attractive for behavioral reasons (procrastination, hyperbolic discounting) that are discussed at length in current economic literature.

1.2 SHORT HISTORY OF ANNUITY MARKETS

Annuities, in one form or another, have been around for more than two thousand years. In Roman times, speculators sold financial instruments called *annua*, or annual stipends. In return for a lump-sum payment, these contracts promised to pay the buyer a fixed yearly payment for life, or sometimes for a specified period or term. The Roman Domitius Ulpianus was one of the first annuity dealers and is credited with creating the first life expectancy table.

During the Middle Ages, lifetime annuities purchased with a single premium became a popular method of funding the nearly constant war that characterized that period. There are records of a form of annuity called a *tontine*, which was an annuity pool in which participants purchased a share and in return received a life annuity. As participants died off, each survivor received a larger payment until, finally, the last survivor received the remaining principal. Part annuity, part lottery, the tontine offered not only security but also a chance to win a handsome jackpot. For a delightful description of tontines see Jennings and Trout (1982).

During the eighteenth century, many European governments sold annuities that provided the security of a lifetime income guaranteed by the state. In England, Parliament enacted hundreds of laws providing for the sale of annuities to fund wars, to provide a stipend to the royal family, and to reward those loyal to it. Fans of Charles Dickens and Jane Austen will know that in the 1700s and 1800s annuities were all the rage in European high society.

The annuity market grew very slowly in the United States. Annuities were mainly purchased to provide income in situations where no other means of providing support were available. They were mostly purchased by lawyers or executors of estates who needed to provide income to a beneficiary as described in a last will and testament.

Until the Great Depression, annuities represented a miniscule share of the total insurance market (only 1.5 percent of life insurance premiums collected in the United States between 1866 and 1920). During and after the Great Depression, investors regarded annuities as relatively safe assets (see, "annuities" in *Wikipedia*).

Today, annuities represent an important line of business for U.S. insurance companies. While annuity payouts represented less than 10 percent of the combined payouts on life insurance and annuities before World War II, they have climbed to about 40 percent today (Brown et al., 2001, chap. 2). The growth of individual annuities has exceeded that of group annuities, reflecting the decline in defined benefits pension plans and the rapid expansion of variable annuities. The growth of variable annuities was accompanied by an expansion of investment options: Starting with diversified common stock portfolios, policies now offer a variety of specialized portfolios of bonds and securities. With the exception of the United Kingdom, European private annuity markets lag behind those in the United States, presumably reflecting a crowding out of private markets by generous public social security systems.

As described in a recent survey of annuity pricing (Cannon and Tonks, 2005), the 1956 Finance Act in the United Kingdom required that accumulated pension assets be converted to annuities upon retirement. This act expanded the annuity market in the United Kingdom (called the *voluntary purchase* market) because of favorable tax treatment and created a much larger *compulsory purchase* annuity market for individuals who opted for a defined contributions personal pension. The prices of annuities are higher in the voluntary market (valued at $111 million) than in the compulsory market (valued at $15 billion), reflecting the higher average age of annuitants in this market. The United Kingdom has annuities whose payout is indexed to consumer prices, as well as nonindexed annuities. Annuities are sold at discounted prices to those who can prove they have "severely impaired lives" (Finkelstein and Poterba, 2002, 2004).

A recent survey of annuity markets around the world (James and Song, 2001) reports increasing and thriving annuity markets in developed and developing countries and calculates the *money's worth* of annuities (expected present value of payouts relative to the annuity's price), indicating surprisingly low adverse selection.

Private annuities in the United States and the United Kingdom are sold by insurance companies. Supply conditions depend upon the availability of assets that provide satisfactory coverage for the obligations of these firms. In both countries, there is a high degree of concentration of annuity providers (Prudential, for example, accounts for 40 percent of new annuity sales in the United Kingdom), but according to Cannon and Tonks (2006), based on money's worth calculations, there is no evidence of monopolistic profits. Life insurers and annuity providers can reduce their exposure to cohort longevity risk by buying longevity bonds (whose coupons fall in line with longevity) or by reinsurance. So far, the supply of longevity bonds is rather limited, but reinsurance is widely practiced.

1.3 REFERENCES TO ACTUARIAL FINANCE

An encyclopedic book of actuarial calculations with different mortality functions is Bowers et al. (1997), published by the Society of Actuaries. Duncan (1952) and Biggs (1969) provide formulas for variable annuities, that is, for annuities with stochastic returns. For an overview of life insurance formulas, see Baldwin (2002). Another useful book with rigorous mathematical derivations is Gerber (1990).

Milevsky's (2006) recent book contains many useful actuarial formulas for specific mortality functions (such as the Gompertz–Makeham function) that provide a good fit with the data. It also considers the implications of stochastic investment returns for annuity pricing, a topic not discussed in this book.

CHAPTER 2

Benchmark Calculations: Savings and Retirement

IN ORDER TO HIGHLIGHT the interaction between the objective of individuals to smooth consumption over lifetime and the savings needed during the working phase of life to finance consumption during retirement, it will be illuminating to calculate some simple numerical examples. These examples assume complete certainty with respect to all relevant variables. Longevity and other uncertainties, the raison d'etre for insurance via annuities, will be introduced subsequently.

Suppose consumption starts at some young age, say 20. Age, denoted z, is taken to be continuous, and age 20 is $z = 0$. The individual works from age M, $M \geq 0$, to an age of retirement, R ($R > M$), and earns 1 unit of income at all ages during the working phase. After retirement, the individual continues to live until age T ($T > R$). Assume that the individual wishes to consume a constant flow, c, while working and a flow of ρc during retirement. Since income is normalized to 1, c is the rate of consumption, and $1 - c$ is the rate of savings when working. Typically, the ratio of consumption during retirement to consumption, during the working phase (called the replacement ratio, when dealing with old-age pension benefits) ρ, is a constant, $0 \leq \rho \leq 1$.

Consumption is constrained by a lifetime budget that equates the present value of consumption to the present value of income:

$$c \int_0^R e^{-rz} \, dz + \rho c \int_R^T e^{-rz} \, dz = \int_M^R e^{-rz} \, dz \qquad (2.1)$$

or

$$c \left[1 - e^{-rR} + \rho(e^{-rR} - e^{-rT}) \right] = e^{-rM} - e^{-rR}, \qquad (2.2)$$

where r is the instantaneous rate of interest.

Table 2.1 displays the rates of consumption, c, and savings, $1 - c$, as well as the level of wealth, W, at retirement,

$$W = \int_M^R e^{rz} \, dz - c \int_0^R e^{rz} \, dz = \frac{1}{r} \left[e^{rR} - e^{rM} - c(e^{rR} - 1) \right], \qquad (2.3)$$

for select values of the parameters: $R = 30$, $T = 45$, $r = .03$, $M = 0, 5$, and $\rho = \frac{1}{2}, \frac{2}{3}$.

TABLE 2.1
Consumption, Savings, and Wealth at Retirement.

	$\rho = \frac{1}{2}$		$\rho = \frac{2}{3}$	
	$M = 0$	$M = 5$	$M = 0$	$M = 5$
c	.89	.68	.86	.66
$1 - c$	.11	.32	.14	.34
W	5.37	10.14	6.91	11.31

The values chosen for ρ take into account that social security (SS) benefits provide (in the United States) a replacement ratio of 25–30 percent for the average participant, hence these calculations show the *additional* savings required to attain a reasonably steady level of consumption.

The above calculations show that individuals who start working early ($M = 0$) should save more than 10 percent of their incomes. A postponement of the work starting age (due, say, to extended education or family circumstances) dramatically raises the required savings rate. Hence the argument that SS systems that provide retirement benefits independent of cumulative contributions *cross-subsidize* late-entry participants (Brown, 2002).[1]

It is easy to incorporate simple forms of uncertainty about survival into these calculations. For example, suppose that the probability of surviving to age z after retirement is $e^{-\alpha(z-R)}$ (no uncertainty about surviving to retirement). With perfect insurance, equation (2.1) and subsequent equations now have *expected* consumption after age R, which means that discounting during retirement is at a rate of $r + \alpha$. For example, when the expected lifetime after retirement is about 10, then $\alpha = .1$. This slightly increases consumption and decreases savings and wealth at retirement in table 2.1.

Note that from (2.1), the elasticity of consumption with respect to longevity is approximately (taking linear expansions)

$$\frac{T}{c} \frac{\partial c}{\partial T} \simeq -\frac{\rho}{(1 - \rho)R/T + \rho} < 0. \tag{2.4}$$

Thus, $(T/c)(\partial c/\partial T) \geq -1$. A 1 percent increase in longevity, holding retirement age constant, leads to a decrease in consumption of a fraction of 1 percent, implying an increase in the savings rate.

---

[1] This problem does not exist in *notional defined contribution* systems.

Similarly, the elasticity of consumption with respect to retirement age is approximately

$$\frac{R}{c}\frac{\partial c}{\partial R} \simeq \frac{1/c - 1 + \rho}{1 - \rho + \rho T/R} > 0. \tag{2.5}$$

For the above values ($R = 30$, $T = 45$, $r = .03$) and $\rho = \frac{1}{2}$, this elasticity is $\frac{3}{4}$. This is lower than the *delayed retirement credit* in the United States, which provides about a 6 percent increase in annual benefits for a 1-year postponement of retirement beyond the normal retirement age, currently at 65.

Finally, the ratios of wealth to income at retirement, W, presented in table 2.1, all in excess of 5, are significantly higher than observed ratios in the United States (Diamond, 1977). This presumably a reflection of shortsightedness, may be one explanation for the high poverty rates among the elderly in the United States.

CHAPTER 3

Survival Functions, Stochastic Dominance, and Changes in Longevity

3.1 SURVIVAL FUNCTIONS

As in chapter 2, age is taken to be a continuous variable, denoted z, whose range is from 0 to maximum lifetime, denoted T. Formally, it is possible to allow $T = \infty$. When considering individual decisions, age 0 should be interpreted as the earliest age at which decisions are undertaken. Uncertainty about longevity, that is, the age of death, is represented by a *survival distribution function*, $F(z)$, which is the probability of survival to age z.

The function $F(z)$ satisfies $F(0) = 1$, $F(T) = 0$, and $F(z)$ strictly decreases in z. We shall assume that $F(z)$ is differentiable and hence that the probability of death at age z, which is the density function of $1 - F(z)$, exists for all z, $f(z) = -dF(z)/dz > 0$, $0 \le z \le T$.

A commonly used survival function is

$$F(z) = \frac{e^{-\alpha z} - e^{-\alpha T}}{1 - e^{-\alpha T}}, 0 \le z \le T, \tag{3.1}$$

where $\alpha > 0$ is a constant. In the limiting case, when $T = \infty$, this is the well-known exponential function $F(z) = e^{-\alpha z}$ (see figure 3.1).

Life expectancy, denoted $\bar{z}$, is defined by

$$\bar{z} = \int_0^T z f(z) \, dz.$$

Integrating by parts,

$$\bar{z} = \int_0^T F(z) \, dz. \tag{3.2}$$

For survival function (3.1), $\bar{z} = (1/\alpha) - (T/(e^{\alpha T} - 1))$. Hence, when $T = \infty$, $\bar{z} = 1/\alpha$. To obtain some notion about parameter values, if life expectancy is 85, then $\alpha = .012$. With this α, the probability of survival to age 100 is $e^{-1.2} = .031$, somewhat higher than the current fraction of surviving 100-year-olds in developed countries.

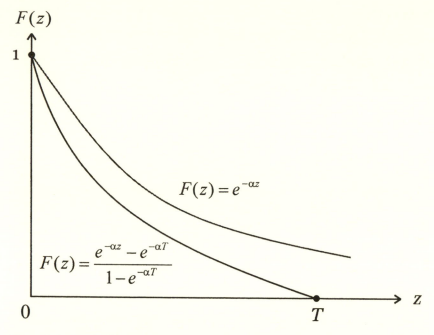

Figure 3.1. Survival functions.

The conditional probability of dying at age z, $f(z)/F(z)$, is termed the *hazard rate* of survival function $F(z)$. For function (3.1), for example, the hazard rate is equal to $\alpha/(1 - e^{\alpha(z-T)})$, which for any finite T increases with z. When $T = \infty$, the hazard rate is constant, equal to α.

It will be useful to formalize the notion that one survival function has a "shorter life span" or "is more risky" than another. The following is a direct application of the theory of stochastic dominance in investment decisions.[1]

Consider two survival functions, $F_i(z)$, $i = 1, 2$.

Definition *(Single crossing or stochastic dominance). The function $F_1(z)$ is said to (strictly) stochastically dominate $F_2(z)$ if the hazard rates satisfy*

$$\frac{f_2(z)}{F_2(z)} > \frac{f_1(z)}{F_1(z)}, \qquad 0 \le z \le T. \tag{3.3}$$

In words, the rate of decrease of survival probabilities,

$$\frac{d \ln F(z)}{dz} = -\frac{f(z)}{F(z)},$$

[1] See, for example, Levy (1998) and the references therein.

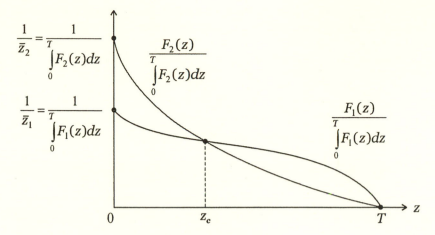

Figure 3.2. $F_1(z)$ stochastically dominates $F_2(z)$.

is smaller at all ages with survival function 1 than with survival function 2.

Two implications of this definition are important. First, consider the functions

$$\frac{F_i(z)}{\bar{z}_i} = \frac{F_i(z)}{\int_0^T F_i(z)\,dz}, \quad 0 \le z \le T, i = 1, 2.$$

Being positive and with their integral over $(0, T)$ equal to 1, they must intersect (cross) at least once over this range. At any such crossing, when

$$\frac{F_1(z)}{\int_0^T F_1(z)\,dz} = \frac{F_2(z)}{\int_0^T F_2(z)\,dz},$$

condition (3.3) implies that

$$\frac{d}{dz}\left(\frac{F_1(z)}{\int_0^T F_1(z)\,dz}\right) > \frac{d}{dz}\left(\frac{F_2(z)}{\int_0^T F_2(z)\,dz}\right).$$

Hence, there can only be a single crossing. That is, there exists an age z_c, $0 < z_c < T$, such that (figure 3.2)

$$\frac{F_1(z)}{\int_0^T F_1(z)\,dz} \; {\textstyle \begin{array}{c} \le \\ = \\ > \end{array}} \; \frac{F_2(z)}{\int_0^T F_2(z)\,dz} \quad \text{as} \quad z \; {\textstyle \begin{array}{c} \le \\ = \\ > \end{array}} \; z_c. \tag{3.4}$$

Intuitively, (3.4) means that the dominant (dominated) distribution has higher (lower) survival rates, relative to life expectancy, at older (younger) ages.

Second, since $F_i(0) = 1$, $i = 1, 2$, it follows from (3.4) that

$$\bar{z}_1 = \int_0^T F_1(z)\,dz > \int_0^T F_2(z)\,dz = \bar{z}_2; \tag{3.5}$$

that is, stochastic dominance implies *higher life expectancy*.

3.2 Changes in Longevity

It will be useful in later chapters to study the effects of changes in longevity. Thus, suppose that survival functions are a function of age and, in addition, a parameter, denoted α, that represents longevity, $F(z, \alpha)$. We take an increase in α to (weakly) decrease (in analogy to the function $e^{-\alpha z}$) survival probabilities at all ages: $\partial F(z, \alpha)/\partial \alpha \leq 0$ (with strict inequality for some z) for all $0 \leq z \leq T$.

How does a change in α affect the hazard rate? Using the previous definitions,

$$\frac{\partial}{\partial \alpha}\left(\frac{f(z, \alpha)}{F(z, \alpha)}\right) = -\frac{\partial \mu(z, \alpha)}{\partial z}. \tag{3.6}$$

where

$$\mu(z, \alpha) = \frac{1}{F(z, \alpha)} \frac{\partial F(z, \alpha)}{\partial \alpha}(< 0)$$

is the *relative* change in $F(z, \alpha)$ due to a small change in α.

It is seen that a decrease in α (increasing survival rates) reduces the hazard rate when it has a proportionately larger effect on survival probabilities at older ages, and vice versa[2] (figure 3.3). This observation will be important when we discuss the effects of changes in longevity on individuals' behavior.

A special case of a change in longevity is when lifetime is finite and known with certainty. Thus, let

$$F(z, \alpha) = \begin{cases} 1, & 0 \leq z \leq T, \\ 0, & z > T, \end{cases} \tag{3.7}$$

---

[2] A sufficient condition for (3.6) to be positive is that $\dfrac{\partial^2 F(z, \alpha)}{\partial \alpha\, \partial z} < 0$. For $F(z, \alpha) = e^{-\alpha z}$, $\dfrac{\partial^2 F(z, \alpha)}{\partial \alpha\, \partial z} \gtrless 0$ as $\alpha z \gtrless 1$. However, $\dfrac{\partial}{\partial \alpha}\left(\dfrac{f(z, \alpha)}{F(z, \alpha)}\right) = 1$ for all z.

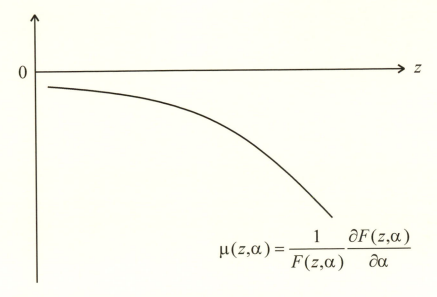

$$\mu(z,\alpha) = \frac{1}{F(z,\alpha)} \frac{\partial F(z,\alpha)}{\partial \alpha}$$

Figure 3.3. An increase in longevity reduces the hazard rate.

where $T = T(\alpha)$ depends negatively on α. Survival is certain until age T. An increase in longevity means in this case simply a lengthening of lifetime, T. The condition in figure 3.3 is satisfied in a discontinuous form: $\partial F(z, \alpha)/\partial \alpha = 0$ for $0 \leq z < T$ and $\partial F(T, \alpha)/\partial \alpha < 0$.

Function (3.1) has two parameters, α and T, that affect longevity in different ways:

$$F(z, \alpha, T) = \frac{e^{-\alpha z} - e^{-\alpha T}}{1 - e^{-\alpha T}}.$$

We can examine separately the effects of a change in α and a change in T (figure 3.4):

$$\frac{\partial F(z, \alpha, T)}{\partial \alpha} = \frac{1 - e^{-\alpha z}}{1 - e^{-\alpha T}} \left(\frac{T}{e^{\alpha T} - 1} - \frac{z}{e^{\alpha z} - 1} \right) < 0, \qquad 0 < z < T$$

$$= 0, \qquad z = 0, \ T, \qquad\qquad (3.8)$$

and

$$\frac{\partial F(z, \alpha, T)}{\partial T} = \frac{\alpha}{e^{\alpha T} - 1} \left(\frac{1 - e^{-\alpha z}}{1 - e^{-\alpha T}} \right) > 0, \qquad 0 < z \leq T$$

$$= 0, \qquad z = 0. \qquad\qquad (3.9)$$

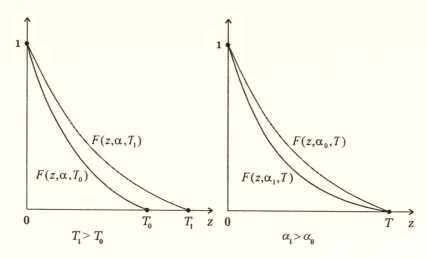

Figure 3.4. Parametric changes for survival function (3.1).

The difference between these two parametric effects on survival rates is that a change in α affects mainly medium ages, while a change in T affects largely older ages.

Note also that, for (3.1), an increase in α raises the hazard rate, while an increase in T reduces the hazard rate. Hence, an increase in longevity that jointly reduces α and raises T unambiguously decreases the hazard rate.

CHAPTER 4

Life Cycle Model with Longevity Risk: First Best and Competitive Equilibrium

Denote consumption at age z by $c(z)$. Utility of consumption, $u(c)$, is assumed to be positive, independent of age, strictly increasing, differentiable, and strictly concave in $c (u(c) > 0,\ u'(c) > 0,\ u''(c) < 0)$.[1] We want to focus on the effects of the availability or absence of an insurance market on consumption and retirement decisions. Thus, we do not model decisions on the intensity of work, assuming that when working the individual provides 1 unit of labor. Disutility of work, $e(z)$, is independent of consumption and increases with age, $e'(z) > 0$.[2] Contingent on survival, individuals work between ages 0 and R, which denotes the chosen retirement age. Our assumptions ensure that, once retired, individuals never return to work.

At this stage, we assume that there is no bequest motive.[3] The individual's objective is to maximize *expected lifetime utility*, denoted by V. With no subjective discount rate (time preference),

$$V = \int_0^T F(z)u(c(z))\,dz - \int_0^R F(z)e(z)\,dz. \tag{4.1}$$

4.1 First Best

We assume that the economy consists of numerous individuals and hence the *law of large numbers* applies. There is no capital, and wages can be carried forward or backward in time at no discount. Let wages (productivity) at age z be denoted $w(z)$. It is assumed that $w(z)$ is continuous for all $0 \leq z \leq T$. With a large number of individuals, the economy's aggregate resource constraint equates expected lifetime

---

[1] Utility after death is taken to be 0. The assumption that $u(c) > 0$ is needed for longevity to be a positive "good." See equation (5.9) below.

[2] Without additive separability, consumption and work decisions are interrelated, with discontinuity in consumption upon retirement.

[3] This is discussed in chapter 11.

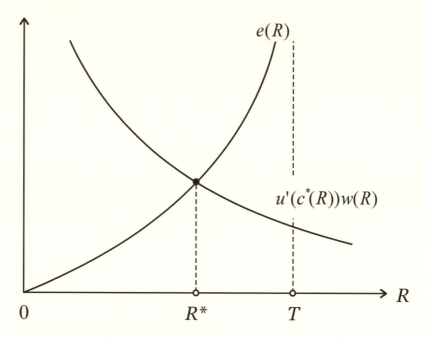

Figure 4.1. Optimum retirement.

consumption to expected lifetime wages:

$$\int_0^T F(z)c(z)\,dz - \int_0^R F(z)w(z)\,dz = 0. \tag{4.2}$$

When $T = \infty$, it is assumed that all feasible paths, $(c(z), R)$, satisfying (4.2) yield finite values of V, equation (4.1). A sufficient condition is for the utility function, $u(c)$, to be bounded above.

Maximization of (4.1) subject to (4.2) yields an optimum constant consumption flow, $c(z) = c^*$, $0 \le z \le T$. The level of c^* depends on the age of retirement. By (4.2),

$$c^* = c^*(R) = \frac{W(R)}{\bar{z}}, \tag{4.3}$$

where $W(R) = \int_0^R F(z)w(z)\,dz$ is expected wages until retirement.

The condition for an optimum interior retirement age is

$$u'(c^*(R))w(R) - e(R) = 0. \tag{4.4}$$

Condition (4.4) states that, at the optimum, the marginal utility from consumption due to a small postponement of retirement is equal to marginal labor disutility. Denote the solution to (4.4) by R^* (figure 4.1).

Sufficient conditions for a unique interior solution, $0 < R^* < T$, are $e(0) = 0$, $e(T) = \infty$, and $w'(R) \leq 0$ for all R.[4] These conditions ensure that the curve $u'(c^*(R))w(R)$ is downward-sloping and hence intersects the curve $e(R)$ at an interior value, $0 < R^* < T$.[5]

Jointly, these assumptions imply that the individual plans to have, if alive, a period of retirement and that their planned retirement age occurs on the downside of life cycle wages.

The first-best allocation $(c^*(R^*), R^*)$ yields optimum expected utility, V^*,

$$V^* = u(c^*(R^*))\bar{z} - \int_0^{R^*} F(z)e(z)\, dz. \qquad (4.5)$$

4.2 Competitive Equilibrium: Full Annuitization

Suppose that the individual can purchase or sell at any age an asset called *annuities*. The quantity of annuities at age z is denoted $a(z)$. A unit of annuities is purchased at a price of 1 and yields an instantaneous return for an age-z holder, contingent on survival, denoted by $r(z)$. In case of death the obligation (entitlement) expires. The amount of annuities can be positive or negative. A positive amount means that the individual is entitled to the returns on annuities written by others (insurance firms or banks), while a negative amount means that the individual has a contingent obligation on loans that expire upon death.

At any age z, the purchase or sale of annuities, $\dot{a}(z) = da(z)/dz$, is determined by the budget dynamics

$$\dot{a}(z) = r(z)a(z) + w(z) - c(z). \qquad (4.6)$$

It is understood that $w(z) = 0$ for $R \leq z \leq T$. Given $w(z)$, $c(z)$, and $a(0) = 0$, the solution to (4.6) is the holdings of annuities at age z:

$$a(z) = \exp\left(\int_0^z r(x)\, dx\right) \int_0^z \exp\left(-\int_0^x r(h)\, dh\right)(w(x) - c(x))\, dx. \quad (4.7)$$

---

[4] Instead of the assumption about labor disutility, it can be assumed that $u'(0) = \infty$ and $u'(\infty) = 0$. The assumption that wages are nonincreasing for all R may be viewed as too strong because in a typical life cycle wages increase and then decrease with age. Strictly, it needs to be assumed that optimum retirement occurs on the downside of wages.

[5] $\dfrac{d\ln(u'(c^*(R))w(R))}{dR} = \dfrac{w'(R)}{w(R)} - \sigma\dfrac{F(R)w(R)}{\int_0^R F(z)w(z)\, dz}$, where $\sigma = -\dfrac{u''(c^*)c^*}{u'(c^*)} > 0$.

Because individuals have no bequest motive, $a(T) = 0$. This implies, by (4.7), that

$$\int_0^T \exp\left(-\int_0^x r(h)\,dh\right)(w(x) - c(x))\,dx = 0. \qquad (4.8)$$

We look for rates of return, $r(z)$, that satisfy the resource constraint (4.2). Comparing (4.8) and (4.2), we see that when

$$r(z) = -\frac{d\ln F(z)}{dz} = \frac{f(z)}{F(z)}, \qquad (4.9)$$

then (4.8) and (4.2) are identical. Condition (4.9), termed the *no-arbitrage condition*, is equivalent to the condition that expected profits are equal to 0: Annuities pay to age-z holders a rate of return that is equal to the hazard rate at this age. This is the fraction of age-z individuals who are expected to die in a short while and, consequently, their annuities will expire. Suppose that in a small interval around some z_0, $f(z)/F(z) > r(z)$. Firms can make a profit by selling annuities to individuals who are around the age of z_0, offering a slightly higher return than the market return, $r(z)$. This still leaves them with a profit because a fraction $f(z)/F(z)$ of these individuals will die and consequently their entitlements as annuity holders will expire. Competition will generate a process of rising rates of return so long as $r(z)$ is lower than $f(z)/F(z)$. The same argument shows that when $f(z)/F(z) < r(z)$, firms incur losses, generating a process of lower returns until (4.9) is satisfied.

Under the no-arbitrage condition, (4.9), the demand for annuities, (4.7), becomes

$$a(z) = \frac{1}{F(z)}\int_0^z F(x)(w(x) - c(x))\,dx$$

$$= \frac{1}{F(z)}\int_0^z F(x)s(x)\,dx, \qquad (4.10)$$

where $s(x) = w(x) - c(x)$ are savings at age x (after age R, $w(x) = 0$ and $s(x) = -c(x)$). It is seen that savings are fully annuitized and hence, in the absence of a bequest motive, total expected lifetime savings, S, are equal to 0: $S = \int_0^T F(x)s(x)\,dx = 0$.[6]

We conclude that when (4.9) is satisfied, and hence (4.8) and (4.2) are identical, the competitive equilibrium yields the first-best solution, $(c^*(R^*), R^*)$.

---

[6] As observed by Sheshinski (1999), this can be implemented by investing savings in a large pension fund that distributes annually the assets of deceased participants to survivors in the same age cohort.

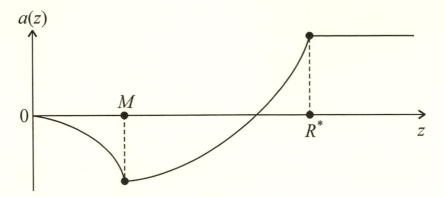

Figure 4.2. Demand for annuities.

4.3 EXAMPLE: EXPONENTIAL SURVIVAL FUNCTION

Let $F(z) = e^{-\alpha z}$, $0 \leq z \leq \infty$. The no-arbitrage condition, (4.9), implies that $r(z) = \alpha$. Suppose that the individual earns a constant wage, w, starting at age $M (\geq 0)$, until retirement at age $R^* (>M)$. Then, consumption, (4.3), is

$$c^* = w \, (e^{-\alpha M} - e^{-\alpha R^*}), \tag{4.11}$$

and the demand for annuities, (4.10), is

$$a(z) = \begin{cases} -\dfrac{w}{\alpha}(e^{-\alpha M} - e^{-\alpha R^*})(e^{\alpha z} - 1), & 0 \leq z \leq M, \\[2ex] \dfrac{w}{\alpha}(e^{\alpha(z-M)} - 1) - \dfrac{w}{\alpha}(e^{-\alpha M} - e^{-\alpha R^*})(e^{\alpha z} - 1), & M \leq z \leq R^*, \\[2ex] \dfrac{w}{\alpha}(e^{-\alpha M} - e^{-\alpha R^*}), & z \geq R^*. \end{cases} \tag{4.12}$$

It is seen (figure 4.2) that early in life the individual sells annuities (takes contingent loans) to finance consumption and then, as earnings start coming in, obligations are reduced and eventually eliminated. The individual purchases an increasing amount of annuities, holding at retirement a positive amount that is maintained indefinitely after retirement.

When $M = 0$, the first phase is absent; the individual holds throughout life a positive amount of annuities (accumulating until retirement and maintained at a constant level thereafter).

4.4 Equivalence of Short-term, Long-term, and Deferred Annuities

With an unchanged survival function, the purchase of a long-term annuity, that is, an annuity that is held and pays a return over a given period (or for the indefinite future) is equivalent to the purchase of a sequence of short-term annuities. Similarly, if the holder of an annuity locks it for a certain duration before starting to receive returns, as is typical of many retirement plans, the actuarially fair discounted price of such an annuity will reflect the probability that the holder will die before the activation of the annuity. Thus, the cumulative returns on an annuity locked in from age 0 to age M are $\exp(\int_0^M r(z)\,dz) = 1 - F(M)$. This is the discounted competitive price for which the annuity will be sold at age 0.

The equivalence of these various pay schemes depends crucially on the absence of any new information obtained by the issuers of annuities on the survival probabilities of customers. In chapter 7 we shall discuss the impact of such information on the annuity market equilibrium.

Appendix

A number of recent studies report a significant reduction (about 13 percent) in the level of consumption after retirement compared to the level before retirement (the *retirement-consumption puzzle*). Several explanations have been offered for this drop. One explanation, put forward by Bernheim et al. (2001), is that workers do not adequately foresee the decline in income associated with retirement. Hurd and Rohwedder (2006), though, provide direct evidence that households have rational forecasts about future income. We want to outline how the life cycle model presented in this chapter can be modified to yield a downward discontinuity in consumption at retirement.

We continue to denote utility of consumption when working by $u(c)$, while utility of consumption when not working is denoted by $v(c)$ (which also satisfies the standard assumptions, $v(c) > 0$, $v'(c) > 0$, $v''(c) < 0$). Expected utility, V, is now

$$V = \int_0^R F(z)u(c(z))\,dz + \int_R^T F(z)v(c(z))\,dz - \int_0^R F(z)e(z)\,dz, \quad (4A.1)$$

while the budget (or resource) constraint is (3.2). The first-order conditions yield optimum constant consumption levels before retirement, c_w^*, and after retirement, c_R^*, which equate marginal utilities of consumption,

$$u'(c_w^*) = v'(c_R^*). \quad (4A.2)$$

If work has a positive effect on the marginal utility of consumption, that is, $u'(c) > v'(c)$ for all c, then it follows from (4A.2) that $c_w^* > c_R^*$.

The condition that determines the optimum retirement age is now

$$u'(c_w^*)w(R) + (u(c_w^*) - v(c_R^*)) = e(R). \quad (4A.3)$$

The left hand side of (4A.3), the benefits (in terms of utility) from a marginal postponement of retirement, now includes an additional term, $u(c_w^*) - v(c_R^*)$, which is the difference in utility, at the optimum, of consumption when working and not working.

Finally, c_w^* and c_R^* satisfy the budget constraint

$$c_w^* \int_0^R F(z) \, dz + c_R^* \int_R^T F(z) \, dz - \int_0^R F(z) w(z) \, dz = 0. \qquad (4A.4)$$

Equations (4A.2)–(4A.4) jointly determine the solution c_w^*, c_R^*, and R^*. Sufficient conditions for uniqueness are $c_w^* - c_R^* - w(R^*) < 0$ at R^* (which clearly holds when individuals save just prior to retirement) and $(v''(c_R^*)/v'(c_R^*)) - (u''(c_w^*)/u'(c_w^*)) > 0$, that is, individuals are more risk averse after retirement.

When $c_w^* > c_R^*$, it follows from (4A.4) that $c_w^* > \int_0^R F(z) w(z) \, dz / \bar{z}$. Now, if it is assumed that $u(c) - v(c) < 0$ for all c, then (since $c_w^* > c_R^*$) it follows, comparing (4A.3) and (3.4), that optimum retirement age, R^*, is now smaller than when $u(c) = v(c)$. If, on the other hand, $u(c) - v(c) > 0$, then it is not possible to establish a priori whether R^* is now larger or smaller. It is important to note that the assumption that leads to the observable pattern, $c_w^* > c_R^*$, does not imply, in itself, the direction of the effect on the optimum retirement age.

CHAPTER 5

Comparative Statics, Discounting,
Partial Annuitization, and No Annuities

5.1 Increase in Wages

Suppose that $w(z)$ is constant, w, for all z. Totally differentiating (4.4) with respect to w, we find the effect of an increase in wages on optimum retirement:

$$\frac{w}{R^*}\frac{dR^*}{dw} = \frac{1-\sigma}{\sigma\dfrac{F(R^*)R^*}{\int_0^{R^*} F(z)\,dz} + \dfrac{e'(R^*)R^*}{e(R^*)}}, \tag{5.1}$$

where

$$\sigma = \sigma(c^*) = -\frac{u''(c^*)c^*}{u'(c^*)} > 0,$$

the *coefficient of relative risk aversion* is evaluated at the optimum consumption level. Hence, $dR^*/dw \gtreqless 0$ as $\sigma \lesseqgtr 1$. For a given retirement age, R^*, an increase in w raises the marginal value of postponing retirement provided consumption is constant, but it also raises consumption, thereby decreasing the marginal utility of consumption and hence the value of this postponement. Which of these opposite effects dominates depends on whether the elasticity of the marginal utility is larger or smaller than unity.

The change in optimum consumption, taking into account the change in the age of retirement, is always positive. By (4.3),

$$\frac{w}{c^*}\frac{dc^*}{dw} = 1 + \frac{F(R^*)R^*}{\int_0^{R^*} F(z)\,dz}\frac{w}{R^*}\frac{dR^*}{dw}$$

$$= \left(\frac{F(R^*)R^*}{\int_0^{R^*} F(z)\,dz} + \frac{e'(R^*)R^*}{e(R^*)}\right)\Bigg/\left(\sigma\frac{F(R^*)R^*}{\int_0^{R^*} F(z)\,dz} + \frac{e'(R^*)R^*}{e(R^*)}\right) > 0. \tag{5.2}$$

Furthermore,

$$\frac{w}{c^*}\frac{dc^*}{dw} \gtreqless 1 \quad \text{as} \quad \sigma \lesseqgtr 1.$$

5.2 Increase in Longevity

As in Chapter 3, let survival functions depend on a parameter, α, that represents longevity, $F(z, \alpha)$. Recall that we take a decrease in α to (weakly) increase survival probabilities at all ages: $\partial F(z, \alpha)/\partial \alpha \leq 0$.

For a given retirement age, how does the change in survival probabilities affect optimum consumption? Differentiating (4.3) partially with respect to α, using the definition of $\bar{z}$,

$$\frac{1}{c^*} \frac{\partial c^*}{\partial \alpha} = \varphi(R^*, \alpha), \tag{5.3}$$

where

$$\varphi(R^*, \alpha) = \frac{\int_0^{R^*} F(z, \alpha) w(z) \mu(z, \alpha) \, dz}{\int_0^{R^*} F(z, \alpha) w(z) \, dz} - \frac{\int_0^{T} F(z, \alpha) \mu(z, \alpha) \, dz}{\int_0^{T} F(z, \alpha) \, dz} \tag{5.4}$$

The condition that ensures that $\varphi(R^*, \alpha) > 0$ for all R^* is that an increase in longevity decreases the hazard rate; that is, expression (3.6) is non-negative:

$$\frac{\partial \mu(z, \alpha)}{\partial z} \leq 0, \qquad 0 \leq z \leq T. \tag{5.5}$$

Under (5.5), $\varphi(0, \alpha) > 0$ and $\varphi(T, 0) > 0$. To see the latter, observe that the integral from 0 to T of

$$\frac{F(z, \alpha) w(z)}{\int_0^T F(z, \alpha) w(z) \, dz} - \frac{F(z, \alpha)}{\int_0^T F(z, \alpha) \, dz}$$

is equal to 0. Hence, this term changes sign at least once over $[0, \ T]$, say at

$$\tilde{z} : \frac{w(\tilde{z})}{\int_0^T F(z, \alpha) w(z) \, dz} - \frac{1}{\int_0^T F(z, \alpha) \, dz} = 0.$$

Using this equality, the partial derivative of this term with respect to z, evaluated at $\tilde{z}$, is $w'(\tilde{z})/w(\tilde{z})\tilde{z} \leq 0$ (by assumption, $w'(z) \leq 0$). Hence, $\tilde{z}$ is unique, implying, by (5.5),

$$\varphi(T, \alpha) > \mu(\tilde{z}, \alpha) \int_0^T \left(\frac{F(z, \alpha) w(z)}{\int_0^T F(z, \alpha) w(z) \, dz} - \frac{F(z, \alpha)}{\int_0^T F(z, \alpha) \, dz} \right) dz = 0. \tag{5.6}$$

Since, under (5.5), $\partial \varphi(R^*, \alpha)/\partial R^* < 0$, it follows that $(1/c^*)(\partial c^*/\partial \alpha) = \varphi(R^*, \alpha) > 0$ for all R^*.

Note that the opposite to the above is also true: Increases in survival rates which are proportionally larger at younger ages, implying an *increase* in the hazard rate, lead to larger optimum consumption (a decrease in savings).

The change in optimum retirement due to a change in α can be found by differentiating (4.4) implicitly with respect to α. In elasticity form,

$$\frac{\alpha}{R^*}\frac{dR^*}{d\alpha} = -\frac{\sigma\dfrac{\alpha}{c^*}\dfrac{\partial c^*}{\partial \alpha}}{\sigma\dfrac{R^*}{c^*}\dfrac{\partial c^*}{\partial R^*} + \dfrac{e'(R^*)R^*}{e(R^*)}}. \tag{5.7}$$

From (4.3),

$$\frac{R^*}{c^*}\frac{\partial c^*}{\partial R^*} = \frac{F(R^*,\alpha)w(R^*)R^*}{\int_0^{R^*} F(z,\alpha)w(z)\,dz}.$$

Since $F(z,\alpha)w(z)$ decreases in z, it is seen that $0 < (R^*/c^*)(\partial c^*/\partial R^*) \le 1$.

We conclude from (5.7) that $dR^*/d\alpha \lesseqgtr 0$ as $\partial c^*/\partial \alpha \gtreqless 0$.

The total change in consumption, taking into account the change in optimum retirement age, is, by (5.7),

$$\frac{dc^*}{d\alpha} = \frac{\partial c^*}{\partial R}\frac{dR^*}{d\alpha} + \frac{\partial c^*}{\partial \alpha} = \left(\frac{\dfrac{e'(R^*)R^*}{e(R^*)}}{\sigma\dfrac{R^*}{c^*}\dfrac{\partial c^*}{\partial R} + \dfrac{e'(R^*)R^*}{e(R^*)}}\right)\frac{\partial c^*}{\partial \alpha}. \tag{5.8}$$

Under condition (5.6), an increase in longevity increases the optimum retirement age, but this compensates only partially for the decrease in consumption due to higher longevity, and hence, $dc^*/d\alpha > 0$.

It was assumed that labor disutility is not affected by longevity. When α affects $e(R,\alpha)$, it is natural to assume that $\partial e(R,\alpha)/\partial \alpha > 0$. The above results, (5.7) and (5.8), have then to be modified (see appendix).

It is of interest to find the effect of a change in α on expected optimum lifetime utility, $V^* = u(c^*)\bar{z} - \int_0^{R^*} F(z,\alpha)e(z)\,dz$.

By the envelope theorem and (4.3) and (4.4),

$$\frac{dV^*}{d\alpha} = \frac{\partial V^*}{\partial \alpha} = [u(c^*) - u'(c^*)c^*]\int_0^T \frac{\partial F(z,\alpha)}{\partial \alpha}\,dz$$

$$+ \int_0^{R^*} [u'(c^*)w(z) - e(z)]\frac{\partial F(z,\alpha)}{\partial \alpha}\,dz. \tag{5.9}$$

Positivity and strict concavity of $u(c)$ together with $u'(c^*)w(z) > e(z)$ for $z \leq R^*$ ensure that an increase in longevity always increases welfare, $dV^*/d\alpha < 0$.[1]

5.3 POSITIVE TIME PREFERENCE AND RATE OF INTEREST

It is useful to observe the modifications required when individuals have a time preference and the shifting of assets (capital) over time carries a positive rate of interest.

Suppose that individuals have a constant positive rate of time preference, $\delta > 0$. Expected utility, (4.1), is rewritten

$$V = \int_0^T e^{-\delta z} F(z) u(c(z)) \, dz - \int_0^R e^{-\delta z} F(z) e(z) \, dz. \qquad (5.10)$$

Assume also that there is a positive constant rate of interest, $\rho > 0$, on (nonannuitized) assets. The aggregate resource constraint, (4.2), is now written

$$\int_0^T e^{-\rho z} F(z) c(z) \, dz - \int_0^R e^{-\rho z} F(z) w(z) \, dz = 0. \qquad (5.11)$$

The expected present values of consumption and of wages are equal. Maximization of (5.10) subject to (5.11) yields optimum consumption, $c^*(z)$, given by[2]

$$c^*(z) = c^*(0) \exp \left(\int_0^z \left(\frac{\rho - \delta}{\sigma} \right) dx \right), \qquad (5.12)$$

where $c^*(0)$ is solved from (5.11) and δ is evaluated at $c^*(z)$. Optimum retirement age is determined, as before, by condition (4.4).

When there is a positive rate of interest on assets, the competitive rate of return on annuities is equal to the rate of interest *plus* the hazard rate. The reason is obvious: The issuers of annuities can invest their proceeds in assets that earn the market rate of interest, and in addition they obtain the hazard rate because their obligations to a fraction of annuity holders, equal to the hazard rate, will expire. Consequently, it is easy to

---

[1] This result depends on our assumption that $u(c) > 0$ independent of age, compared to zero utility at death ("The pleasures of life are worth nothing if one is not alive to experience them," Cutler et al. (2006)). In discussions of investments in life-extending treatments this assumption has at times been questioned.

[2] The first-order condition for an interior maximum is $e^{-\delta z} u'(c^*(z)) = \lambda e^{-\rho z}$, where $\lambda = u'(c^*(0)) > 0$. Differentiating this condition totally with respect to z yields (5.12).

demonstrate that individuals (unlike firms) do not hold nonannuitized assets.

Let the level of nonannuitized assets held at age z be denoted by $b(z)$. These assets, not being annuities that are contingent on survival, must be non-negative if the individual is not to die in debt: $b(z) \geq 0$. The budget dynamics, (4.6), are now written

$$\dot{a}(z) = (\rho + r(z))a(z) + \rho b(z) + w(z) - c(z) - \dot{b}(z). \qquad (5.13)$$

Multiplying (4.13) by $e^{-\rho z}F(z)$ and integrating by parts, we obtain

$$\int_0^T e^{-\rho z}F(z)\,(w(z) - c(z))\,dz - \int_0^T e^{-\rho z}f(z)b(z)\,dz = 0, \qquad (5.14)$$

having used the no-arbitrage condition $r(z) = f(z)/F(z)$. Since $b(z) \geq 0$, clearly the individual sets $b(z) = 0$ for all z. This is the stark proposition first put forward by Yaari (1965): *When individuals face only longevity risks, their savings should be fully annuitized.* As noted above, this result can be attained when individuals invest all their savings in a large pension fund that invests in the market and distributes the market returns annually among the surviving members of each age cohort.

5.4 PARTIAL ANNUITIZATION: NO SHORT-TERM ANNUITY MARKET

Many practical questions about annuitization are concerned with partial annuitization. Of course, a bequest motive leads individuals to devote some resources for this purpose (through the purchase of life insurance or annuities that provide a bequest option. See chapter 11). Still, following the previous discussion, it is optimal to annuitize all remaining assets, a behavior that is not observed in practice.

One explanation given for holding nonannuitized assets for consumption purposes (Davidoff, Brown, and Diamond, 2005) is that often short-term transactions in annuities are not available and the gap between the optimum consumption trajectory and the flow of annuity payouts leads to the holding of other assets. While no apparent reason seems to justify these constraints, it is easy to demonstrate that they may indeed lead to positive holdings of nonannuitized assets.

For our purpose it suffices to take a special case of the previous section. Consider an individual on the verge of retirement, with assets W that can be annuitized, a, or kept in other forms, $b : a + b = W$. Once acquired, the chosen amount of annuities cannot be changed. Each annuity pays a constant flow of payments, γ, while the annuitant is alive, while other assets pay a fixed return of ρ. In equilibrium, of

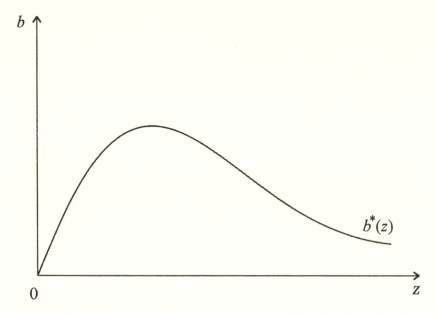

Figure 5.1. Optimum nonannuitized assets.

course, $\gamma = 1 \Big/ \int_0^T F(z)e^{-\rho z}\,dz$. The dynamic budget constraint is

$$\dot{b}(z) = \gamma a + \rho b(z) - c(z), \tag{5.15}$$

with solution

$$b(z) = e^{\rho z}\left[\int_0^z e^{-\rho x}(\gamma a - c(x))\,dx + W - a\right]. \tag{5.16}$$

The amount of $b(z)$ changes with age, depending on the consumption path. The only constraint is that $b(z) \geq 0$ for all z, $0 \leq z \leq T$. Hence, $W - a \geq 0$.

For simplicity, consider the special case $\sigma = 1$ ($u(c) = \ln c$), $\delta = 0$, $T = \infty$, and $F(z) = e^{-\alpha z}$. For this case, $\gamma = \alpha + \rho$. Maximization of expected utility subject to (5.15) yields optimum consumption $c^*(z) = c^*(0)e^{(\rho - \alpha)z}$. Assume that $\rho - \alpha > 0$, implying that consumption rises with age. Solve for $c^*(0)$ from (5.16), setting $\lim_{z \to \infty} b(z)e^{-\rho z} = 0$. Since $b(0) \geq 0$, it is optimum to set $b(0) = 0$ and $a = W$, or $c^*(0) = \alpha((\rho + \alpha)/\rho)\,W$. Substituting in (5.16) we obtain the optimum path, $b^*(z)$. It is now seen from (5.15) that $\dot{b}^*(0) = ((\rho - \alpha)/\rho)(\rho + \alpha)W > 0$. Nonannuitized assets accumulate and then decumulate to support the optimum consumption trajectory (figure 5.1).

5.5 Partial Annuitization: Low Returns on Annuities

Cannon and Tonks (2005) observe that the issuers of annuities (insurance firms) invest their assets, for reasons of liquidity and risk, mainly in bonds that yield a lower return than equities. While the reasons given for this policy are rather weak (and as annuity markets grow, insurance firms are expected to hold more balanced portfolios), this may be another explanation why individuals annuitize only later in life, holding nonannuitized assets at early ages.

To see this, let annuities have a rate of return of $\rho_0 + r(z)$, while nonannuitized assets yield a return of ρ, $\rho > \rho_0$. The budget constraint (5.13) now becomes

$$\dot{a}(z) = (\rho_0 + r)a(z) + \rho b(z) + w(z) - c(z) - \dot{b}(z). \tag{5.17}$$

Multiplying both sides of (5.17) by $e^{-\rho_0 z} F(z)$ and integrating by parts yields

$$\int_0^T e^{-\rho_0 z} F(z)(w(z) - c(z)) \, dz - \int_0^T [r(z) - (\rho - \rho_0)]e^{-\rho_0 z} F(z)b(z) \, dz. \tag{5.18}$$

Recall that $b(z) \geq 0$, $0 \leq z \leq T$. If the hazard rate, $r(z)$, increases with age so that

$$r(z) - (\rho - \rho_0) \lesseqgtr 0 \quad \text{as} \quad z \lesseqgtr z_c, \tag{5.19}$$

then the individual's optimum policy is to invest all assets in b up to age z_c, switching to annuities afterward.

5.6 Length of Life and Retirement

We have seen, in (5.7), that under reasonable conditions for the age profile of changes in longevity, optimum retirement increases with longevity. Recent increases in longevity have largely been concentrated in very old ages (see Cutler, 2004). It is therefore of interest to examine how optimum retirement responds to a steady increase in the length of life.

It is simplest to consider a particular case, (3.7), with no uncertainty and a finite lifetime. With a positive time preference and rate of interest, optimum consumption is given by (5.12), and $c^*(0)$ is determined by condition (5.11) with $F(z) = 1$, $0 \leq z \leq T$:

$$c^*(0) \int_0^T \exp\left(\int_0^z \left(\frac{(1-\sigma)}{\sigma}\rho - \frac{\delta}{\sigma}\right) dx\right) dz - \int_0^{R^*} e^{-\rho z} w(z) \, dz = 0. \tag{5.20}$$

Jointly with the condition for optimum retirement,

$$u'\left(c^*(0)\exp\left(\int_0^{R*}\frac{(\rho-\delta)}{\sigma}\,dx\right)\right)w(R^*)=e(R^*), \tag{5.21}$$

equations (5.15) and (5.21) determine the optimum $(c^*(0),\ R^*)$, which depend on the length of life, T. We are particularly interested in the dependence of R^* on T as it becomes very large. For simplicity, assume that $\sigma=\sigma(c^*(x))$ is constant. Differentiating (5.21) totally with respect to T and inserting the proper expressions from (5.20), we obtain

$$\frac{dR^*}{dT}=\begin{cases}\dfrac{1}{A}\left(\dfrac{(1-\sigma)\rho-\delta}{1-\exp\left(-\frac{1}{\sigma}((1-\sigma)\rho-\delta)T\right)}\right), & (1-\sigma)\rho-\delta\neq0,\\[20pt]\dfrac{\sigma}{AT}, & (1-\sigma)\rho-\delta=0,\end{cases} \tag{5.22}$$

where

$$A=\sigma\frac{e^{-\rho R^*}w(R^*)}{\int_0^{R^*}e^{-\rho z}w(z)\,dz}+\rho-\delta-\frac{w'(R^*)}{w(R^*)}+\frac{e'(R^*)}{e(R^*)}. \tag{5.23}$$

Expression A is positive by the second-order condition for the optimum R^*. Hence, $dR^*/dT>0$. Assume that $\lim_{T\to\infty}A$ is finite, say, $\bar{A}$. Then, from (5.22),

$$\lim_{T\to\infty}\frac{dR^*}{dT}=\begin{cases}\dfrac{1}{\bar{A}}((1-\sigma)\rho-\delta), & (1-\sigma)\rho-\delta>0,\\[14pt]0, & (1-\sigma)\rho-\delta\leq0.\end{cases} \tag{5.24}$$

Thus, when $\sigma\leq1$, optimum retirement age may increase indefinitely as life expectancy rises, provided the rate of time preference is small. When this condition is not satisfied, then optimum retirement approaches a finite age.

This is seen most clearly when wages and labor disutility are assumed constant, $w(z)=w$, $e(z)=e$, and $\rho=\delta>0$. From (5.20) and (5.21), R^* is then determined by the condition

$$u'\left(\frac{w(1-e^{-\rho R^*})}{1-e^{-\rho T}}\right)w=e \tag{5.25}$$

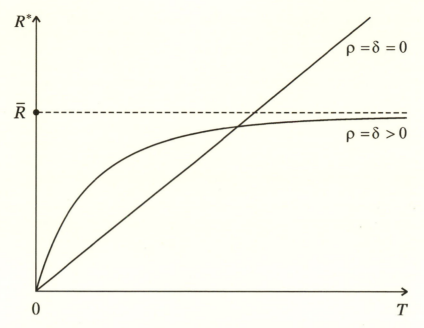

Figure 5.2. Optimum retirement age and length of life ($\overline{R}$ is defined by $u'\,(w(1 - e^{-\rho \overline{R}}))w = e$).

(assuming that the parameters w and e yield an interior solution, $R^* < T$). On the other hand, when $\rho = \delta = 0$, (5.21) becomes

$$u'\left(\frac{wR^*}{T}\right) w = e. \qquad (5.26)$$

With positive discounting, as T becomes large, optimum retirement approaches a finite age, while with no discounting R^*/T remains constant (figure 5.2).

The reason for the difference in the pattern of optimum retirement is straightforward. Without discounting, the importance of a marginal increase in the length of life does not diminish even at high levels of longevity and, accordingly, the individual adjusts retirement to maintain consumption intact. With discounting, the importance of a marginal increase in the length of life diminishes as this change is more distant. Accordingly, the responses of optimum consumption and retirement become negligible and eventually vanish. Subsequently, we shall continue to assume that $\rho = \delta = 0$.

The discussion above, concerning different patterns of optimum retirement response to increasing longevity, is of great practical importance. Many countries have recently raised the normal retirement age (NRA) for receiving social security benefits: In the United States the NRA will reach 67 in 2011, up from 65. Other countries, such as France, Germany, and Israel have also raised their SS retirement ages to 67. In all these cases, postponement of eligibility for "normal" SS benefits seems to be primarily motivated by the long-term solvency needs of the SS systems rather than by consumer welfare considerations. The above analysis points out that in designing future retirement ages for SS systems, consumer preference considerations may provide widely different outcomes. In particular, when the rise in optimum retirement age tapers off as life expectancy rises, this will exacerbate the financial constraints of SS systems, requiring a combination of a reduction of benefits and an increase in contributions.

5.7 Optimum Without Annuities

Suppose that there is no market for annuities but that individuals can save in other assets and use accumulated savings for consumption. Denote the level of these assets at age z by $b(z)$. These assets yield no return. Precluding individuals from dying with debt implies that they cannot incur debt at any age; that is, $b(z) \geq 0$ for all $0 \leq z \leq T$.

The dynamics of the budget constraint are thus

$$\dot{b}(z) = w(z) - c(z), \tag{5.27}$$

where $\dot{b}(z)$ is current savings, positive or negative. The non-negativity constraint on $b(z)$ is written

$$b(z) = \int_0^z (w(x) - c(x))\, dx \geq 0, \qquad 0 \leq z \leq T. \tag{5.28}$$

(Again, it is understood that $w(z) = 0$ for $z \geq R$). Having no bequest motive, the individual plans not to leave any assets at age T[3]:

$$b(T) = \int_0^T (w(z) - c(z))\, dz = 0. \tag{5.29}$$

Assuming that assets (at the optimum) are strictly positive at all ages (and hence (5.28) is nonbinding), maximization of (4.1) subject to (5.29) yields the first-order condition

$$F(z)u'(c(z)) - \lambda = 0, \tag{5.30}$$

[3] Death at any earlier age, $z < T$, may leave a positive amount of unintended bequests, $b(z) > 0$. By assumption, this has no value to the individual, but for aggregate analysis this has to be taken into account.

where $\lambda = u'(c(0))$. In the absence of insurance, optimum consumption requires that the expected marginal utility of consumption be constant at all ages.

Denote the solution to (5.29) and (5.30) by $\hat{c}(z)$. Implicitly differentiating (5.30),

$$\frac{\hat{c}(z)}{\hat{c}(z)} = -\frac{1}{\sigma}\frac{f(z)}{F(z)} < 0, \tag{5.31}$$

where $\sigma = \sigma(z)$ is evaluated at $\hat{c}(z)$. Hence,

$$\hat{c}(z) = \hat{c}(0)\exp\left(-\int_0^z \frac{1}{\sigma}\frac{f(x)}{F(x)}\,dx\right), \tag{5.32}$$

where $\hat{c}(0)$ is determined by (5.29):

$$\hat{c}(0) = \frac{\int_0^R w(z)\,dz}{\int_0^T \exp\left(-\int_0^z \frac{1}{\sigma}\frac{f(x)}{F(x)}\,dx\right)dz} \tag{5.33}$$

Optimum consumption *decreases* with age, its rate of decline being equal to the product of the inverse of the coefficient of relative risk aversion and the hazard rate.

Optimum retirement age, $\hat{R}$, is determined by the same condition as before:

$$u'(\hat{c}(\hat{R}))w(\hat{R}) - e(\hat{R}) = 0. \tag{5.34}$$

Unlike the case with full annuitization, optimum retirement without annuitization depends on the risk attitude of the individual, represented by the coefficient of relative risk aversion. In some simple cases one can determine whether retirement age without annuities, $\hat{R}$, is larger or smaller than retirement age with annuitization, R^*, (4.4). For example, let $\sigma = 1$ ($u(c) = \ln c$). Then

$$\int_0^T \exp\left(-\int_0^z \frac{1}{\sigma}\frac{f(x)}{F(x)}\,dx\right)dz = \int_0^T F(z)\,dz$$

(since $f(z)/F(z) = -d\ln F(z)/dz$), and

$$\exp\left(-\int_0^R \frac{1}{\sigma}\frac{f(x)}{F(x)}\,dx\right) = F(R).$$

It follows now from (5.32) and (5.33) that, for any R,

$$\hat{c}(R) = \frac{\left(\int_0^R w(z)\,dz\right) F(R)}{\int_0^T F(z)\,dz} < \frac{\int_0^R F(z)w(z)\,dz}{\int_0^R F(z)\,dz} = c^*(R). \qquad (5.35)$$

Comparing (5.35) and (4.4), we conclude that $R^* < \hat{R}$.

Finally, we wish to compare the level of welfare with and without annuitization, V and $\hat{V}$, respectively. Optimum expected lifetime utility in the absence of annuitization, $\hat{V}$, is $\hat{V} = \int_0^T F(z)u(\hat{c}(z))\,dz - \int_0^{\hat{R}} F(z)e(z)\,dz$.

Multiplying (5.27) by $F(z)$ and integrating by parts, using $b(0) = b(T) = 0$,

$$\int_0^T f(z)b(z)\,dz = \int_0^T F(z)(w(z) - \hat{c}(z))\,dz > 0. \qquad (5.36)$$

In view of (5.36), there exists a positive number $k, k > 1$ such that $\int_0^T F(z)(w(z) - k\hat{c}(z))\,dz = 0$. Clearly, the consumption path $k\hat{c}(z)$ strictly dominates the path $\hat{c}(z)$ and satisfies the same budget constraint as the first best, c^* (with the same $\hat{R}$). Since the pair (c^*, R^*) maximizes utility under this budget constraint, necessarily $V^* > \hat{V}$.

It should be pointed out that, unlike the analysis of a competitive annuity market, the analysis of individual behavior in the absence of such a market cannot readily be carried over to analyze market equilibrium. The reason is that in the absence of perfect pooling of longevity risks, individuals leave *unintended bequests*. The level of bequests depends on the age at death and hence is random. For an elaboration of the required stochastic long-term (ergodic) analysis of these unintended bequests (and endowments) see chapter 12.

5.8 No Annuities: Risk Pooling by Couples

It has been observed by Kotlikoff and Spivak (1981) that, in the absence of an annuity market, couples who jointly choose their consumption path share longevity risks and hence can partially self-insure against these risks. The argument can be explained by a simple two-period example of a pair of individuals who have independent and identical survival probabilities.[4]

A single individual who lives one period and with probability p, $0 \le p \le 1$, two periods, has an endowment of W, and chooses

---

[4] Using dynamic programming, the analysis can be generalized to many periods and, in the limit, to continuous time.

consumption so as to maximize expected utility $V = u(c_0) + pu(c_1)$, where $c_i \geq 0$ is consumption in period i, $i = 0, 1$. The budget constraint is $c_0 + c_1 = W$. Denote optimum consumption by $(\hat{c}_0, \hat{c}_1)$, and the corresponding optimum expected utility by $\hat{V}$. Now consider two individuals with identical utility functions who maximize the expected sum of their utilities. Since utilities are concave, the couple consumes equal amounts when both are alive. Assume that each individual has the same independent survival probability, p. The couple maximizes the family's expected utility, $2V^c = 2u(c_0) + 2p^2u(c_1/2) + 2p(1 - p)u(c_1)$, where c_0 is per-capita consumption in the first period and c_1 is *total* consumption in the second period. The second term is the sum of the expected utilities of two surviving individuals, while the third is the expected utility of one survivor. The budget constraint is $2c_0 + c_1 = 2W$. Denote optimum consumption by $(\hat{c}_0^c, \hat{c}_1^c)$ and optimum expected utility by $\hat{V}^c$. Note that while $\hat{c}_0^c$ is first-period per-capita consumption, second-period per-capita consumption is $\hat{c}_1^c/2$ or $\hat{c}_1^c$.

It is easy to show that for the couple, each individual's optimum expected utility is larger than that of the single individual. Example: $u(c) = \ln c$. Then $\hat{V} = (1+p)\ln(W/1 + p) + p \ln p$, and $\hat{V}^c = \hat{V} + p(1-p) \ln 2$.[5] The improvement, $\hat{V}^c > \hat{V}$, is entirely due to the pooling of longevity risks.

5.9 Welfare Value of an Annuity Market

In order to measure in money terms how much the availability of an annuity market is worth to the individual, consider the following hypothetical experiment. Suppose that an individual who has no access to an annuity market is provided with a positive exogenous endowment, denoted $A > 0$. Hence his budget constraint becomes

$$A = \int_0^T \hat{c}(z)\, dz - \int_0^{\hat{R}} w(z)\, dz. \tag{5.37}$$

Optimum consumption, $\hat{c}(z)$, age of retirement, $\hat{R}$, and expected utility, $\hat{V}$, all now depend on A, with $\hat{V}(A)$ strictly increasing in A. Let A^* be the level of A that yields the same expected utility to the individual in the absence of annuities as the expected utility with full annuitization, $\hat{V}(A^*) = V^*$. We call A^* the *annuity equivalent level of assets*.

---

[5] Note that $(\hat{c}_1 - \hat{c}_0)/\hat{c}_0 = -(1 - p)$, the decrease in per-capita optimum consumption is equal to the hazard rate, as derived in the previous general analysis (with $\sigma = 1$), while $(\hat{c}_1^c - \hat{c}_0^c)/\hat{c}_0^c = -(1 - p) + p$ is a smaller decrease (or even an increase) because second-period optimum per-capita consumption is either $\hat{c}_1^c/2$ or $\hat{c}_1^c$.

Parametric calculations (e.g., $T = \infty$, $u'(c) = c^{-\sigma}$, $F(z) = e^{-\alpha z}$, $\alpha = \frac{1}{80}$, $w(z) = 1$, and $e(z) = 2$) yield annuity equivalent values for A^* between $\frac{1}{3}wR^*$ and $\frac{2}{5}wR^*$ (between $\frac{1}{3}$ and $\frac{2}{5}$ of lifetime wages) for values of σ between 1 and 2. These calculations highlight the important contribution to individual welfare of having access to an annuity market.

5.10 Example: Exponential Survival Function

As before, let $F(z, \alpha) = e^{-\alpha z}$ and assume a constant wage rate: $w(z) = w$. Then (4.3) becomes

$$c^* = w(1 - e^{-\alpha R^*}). \tag{5.38}$$

From (5.34) and (4.4) we now derive

$$\frac{\alpha}{R^*} \frac{dR^*}{d\alpha} = -\frac{\sigma}{\sigma + \dfrac{e'(R^*)R^*}{e(R^*)} \left(\dfrac{e^{\alpha R^*} - 1}{\alpha R^*} \right)} \tag{5.39}$$

and

$$\frac{\alpha}{c^*} \frac{dc^*}{d\alpha} = \frac{\alpha R^*}{e^{\alpha R^*} - 1} \left(1 + \frac{\alpha}{R^*} \frac{dR^*}{d\alpha} \right) \tag{5.40}$$

Clearly,

$$-1 \leq \frac{\alpha}{R^*} \frac{dR^*}{d\alpha} \leq 0 \quad \text{and} \quad 0 \leq \frac{\alpha}{c^*} \frac{dc^*}{d\alpha} \leq 1.$$

Suppose further that $u(c) = \ln c$. Optimum retirement is now determined by the condition

$$\frac{1}{1 - e^{-\alpha R^*}} = e(R^*). \tag{5.41}$$

With the same survival and utility functions but in the absence of a market for annuities, (5.32)–(5.34) entail optimum consumption, $\hat{c}(z)$, and age of retirement, $\hat{R}$, satisfying

$$\hat{c}(z) = w\alpha \hat{R} e^{-\alpha z}, \tag{5.42}$$

$$\frac{1}{\alpha \hat{R}} e^{\alpha \hat{R}} = e(\hat{R}). \tag{5.43}$$

A sufficient condition for (5.43) to have a unique solution is that the left hand side strictly decreases with $\hat{R}$. This holds when $\hat{R} < 1/\alpha$, that is, optimum retirement age is lower than expected lifetime (which is reasonable, though certainly not necessary).

Comparing (5.41) and (5.43), it is seen that $R^* < \hat{R}$ (figure 5.3).

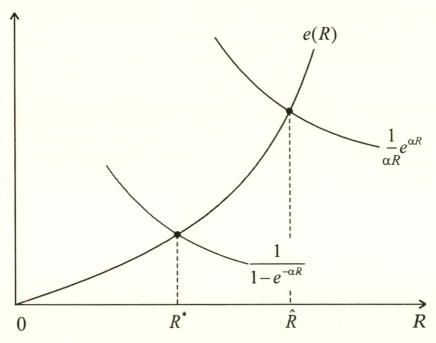

Figure 5.3. Optimum retirement with and without annuities.

Appendix

It seems natural that an increase in longevity (typically reflecting improved health) decreases labor disutility. Thus, assume that $e = e(z, \alpha)$, with $\partial e(z, \alpha)/\partial \alpha > 0$. Expressions (5.7) and (5.8) now become:

$$\frac{\alpha}{R^*} \frac{dR^*}{d\alpha} = -\frac{\sigma \dfrac{\alpha}{c^*} \dfrac{\partial c^*}{\partial \alpha} + \dfrac{\alpha}{e(R^*, \alpha)} \dfrac{\partial e(R^*, \alpha)}{\partial \alpha}}{\sigma \dfrac{R^*}{c^*} \dfrac{\partial c^*}{\partial R^*} + \dfrac{\partial e(R^*, \alpha)}{\partial R^*} \dfrac{R^*}{e(R^*, \alpha)}} \tag{5A.1}$$

and

$$\frac{dc^*}{d\alpha} = \frac{\left(\dfrac{\partial e(R^*, \alpha)}{\partial R^*} \dfrac{R^*}{e(R^*, \alpha)} \right) \dfrac{\alpha}{c^*} \dfrac{\partial c^*}{\partial \alpha} - \left(\dfrac{R^*}{c^*} \dfrac{\partial c^*}{\partial R^*} \right) \dfrac{\alpha}{e(R^*, \alpha)} \dfrac{\partial e(R^*, \alpha)}{\partial \alpha}}{\sigma \dfrac{R^*}{c^*} \dfrac{\partial c^*}{\partial R^*} + \dfrac{\partial e(R^*, \alpha)}{\partial R^*} \dfrac{R^*}{e(R^*, \alpha)}}. \tag{5A.2}$$

Under condition (5.6), the decrease in R^* as α increases is now strengthened, while the (total) effect on consumption may be positive or negative, depending upon whether the increase in consumption at a given retirement age dominates the effect of increased labor disutility.

CHAPTER 6

Subjective Beliefs and Survival Probabilities

6.1 Deviations of Subjective from Observed Frequencies

It has been assumed that individuals, when forming their consumption and retirement plans, have correct expectations about their survival probabilities at all ages. A series of studies (Hurd, McFadden, and Gan, 2003; Hurd, McFadden, and Merrill, 1999; Hurd, Smith, and Zissimopoulos, 2002; Hurd and McGarry, 1993; Manski, 1993) have tested this assumption and examined possible predictors of these beliefs (education, income) using health and retirement surveys. They find that, overall, subjective probabilities aggregate well into observed frequencies, although in the older age groups they find significant deviations of subjective survival probabilities compared with actuarial life table rates (Hurd, McFadden, and Gan, 1998). We shall now inquire how such deviations of survival beliefs from observed (cohort) survival frequencies affect behavior.

Quasi-hyperbolic discounting (Laibson, 1997) is analogous to the use of subjective survival functions that deviate from observed survival frequencies. Laibson views individuals as having a future self-control problem that they realize and take into account in their current decisions. Specifically, "early selves" expect "later selves" to apply excessive time discount rates leading to lower savings and to a "distorted" chosen retirement age, from the point of view of the early individuals (Diamond and Koszegi, 2003). In the absence of commitment devices, the only way to influence later decisions is via changes in the transfer of assets from early to later selves. In our context, this is a case in which individuals apply later in life overly pessimistic survival functions. Sophisticated early individuals take this into account when deciding on their savings and annuity purchases. A number of empirical studies by Laibson and coworkers (Angeletos et al., 2001; Laibson, 2003; Choi et al., 2005, 2006) seem to support this game-theoretic modeling.

6.2 Behavioral Effects

Let $G(z)$ be the individual's subjective survival function, which may deviate from the "true" survival function, $F(z)$. The market for annuities satisfies the no-arbitrage condition; that is, the rate of return on annuities at age z, $r(z)$, is equal to F's hazard rate. Assume, in the spirit of the behavioral studies cited above, that individuals are too pessimistic; that is, the conceived hazard rate, $r_s(z)$, is larger than the market rate of return. Thus,

$$r_s(z) = -\frac{1}{G(z)}\frac{dG(z)}{dz}$$

is assumed to be larger than $r(z)$ for all z.

Maximization of expected utility,

$$V = \int_0^T G(z)u(c(z))\,dz - \int_0^R G(z)e(z)\,dz, \qquad (6.1)$$

subject to the budget constraint (5.2), yields an optimum consumption path, $\hat{c}(z)$,

$$\hat{c}(z) = \hat{c}(0)\exp\left(\int_0^z \frac{1}{\sigma}(r(x) - r_s(x)\,dx\right)dz, \qquad (6.2)$$

where $\sigma = \sigma(x)$, the coefficient of relative risk aversion, is evaluated at $\hat{c}(x)$, and $\hat{c}(0)$ is obtained from the lifetime budget constraint (5.2):

$$\hat{c}(0) = \frac{\int_0^R F(z)w(z)\,dz}{\int_0^T F(z)\exp\left(\int_0^z \frac{1}{\sigma}(r(x) - r_s(x))\,dx\right)dz}. \qquad (6.3)$$

Given our assumption that $r_s(z) - r(z) > 0$ for all z, consumption decreases with age (it increases when $r_s(z) - r(z) < 0$). A higher coefficient of relative risk aversion tends to mitigate the decrease in consumption across ages. Optimum retirement, $\hat{R}$, satisfies the same condition as before:

$$u'(\hat{c}(\hat{R}))w(\hat{R}) - e(\hat{R}) = 0. \qquad (6.4)$$

Conditions (6.2)–(6.4) jointly determine optimum consumption and retirement age.

Comparing first-best consumption c^*, (4.3), with (6.2)–(6.3), we see that

$$\hat{c}(R) \gtreqless c^*(R) \iff \exp\left(\int_0^R \frac{1}{\sigma}(r(z) - r_s(z))dz\right)$$

$$\lesseqgtr \frac{\int_0^T F(z)\exp\left(\int_0^z \frac{1}{\sigma}(r(x) - r_s(x))dx\right)}{\int_0^T F(z)\,dz}. \qquad (6.5)$$

Clearly, at $R = 0$, $\hat{c}(0) > c^*(0)$, while at $R = T$, $\hat{c}(T) < c^*(T)$ (figure 6.1). It is therefore impossible to determine whether $\hat{R}$ is larger or smaller than R^*.

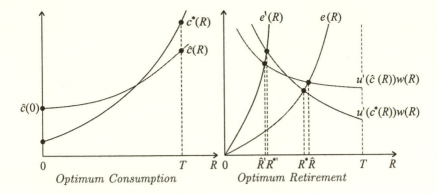

Figure 6.1. Subjective beliefs and optimum retirement.

When beliefs about survival probabilities are more pessimistic than observed frequencies, individuals tend to shift consumption to early ages. Consequently, the benefits of a marginal postponement of retirement are larger if retirement is contemplated at a relatively old age (with low consumption and hence high marginal utility), leading to a higher retirement age compared to the first-best. The opposite effect applies when retirement is contemplated for a relatively early age.

6.3 EXPONENTIAL EXAMPLE

Let $u(c) = \ln c$, $F(z) = e^{-\alpha z}$, and $G(z) = e^{-\beta z}$, $z \geq 0$; α and β are (positive) constants, $\alpha < \beta$. Assume also that the wage rate is constant, w. Then

$$\hat{c}(z) = \frac{\beta w}{\alpha}(1 - e^{-\alpha R})e^{(\alpha - \beta)z}. \tag{6.6}$$

The demand for annuities, $\hat{a}(z)$, (4.7), is now

$$\hat{a}(z) = \begin{cases} \dfrac{w}{\alpha}\left[e^{(\alpha-\beta)z}(1 - e^{-\alpha R}) - (1 - e^{-\alpha(R-z)})\right], & z \leq R, \\[2mm] \dfrac{w}{\alpha}e^{(\alpha-\beta)z}(1 - e^{-\alpha R}), & z > R. \end{cases} \tag{6.7}$$

When $\alpha - \beta < 0$, the individual initially purchases a smaller amount of annuities than in the first-best case, $\alpha = \beta$, reflecting the higher consumption (hence lower savings) at early ages. After retirement, the amount of annuities decreases, reflecting the need to finance lower consumption.

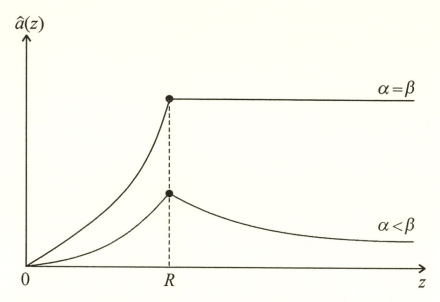

Figure 6.2. Demand for annuities under pessimistic beliefs.

Figure 6.2 has $\hat{a}(z)$ and $a^*(z)$ drawn for the same retirement age. The pattern displays the purchase of a smaller amount of annuities early in life because of overly pessimistic beliefs about survival probabilities (a form of *short-sightedness*). It may provide one explanation of the observed small demand for annuities by young cohorts (the average age of private annuity holders in the United States is 62).

6.4 PRESENT AND FUTURE SELVES

Laibson (1997) argued that individuals realize that they have a self-control problem and take it into account in their decisions. A variation of the previous model can highlight this game-theoretic conflict between earlier selves who know that later selves will make erroneous decisions from their point of view.

Suppose that early in life individuals expect that becuase of overly pessimistic survival prospects, future decision makers (selves) will accelerate consumption and, from the point of view of the early selves, will make erroneous decisions about retirement age (see Diamond and Köszegi, 2003). Early selves can affect future selves through changes in the level of annuities that they purchase early in life.

Suppose that at age $M > 0$, well before retirement age, R, an individual decides on a consumption path and on a retirement age according to a survival function $G(z)$, $z \geq M$. In contrast, the market rate of return on annuities follows the survival function $F(z)$.

Thus, the "age-M self" maximizes expected utility, V_M^1 :

$$V_M^1 = \int_M^\infty G(z)u(c(z))\,dz - \int_M^R G(z)e(z)\,dz, \qquad (6.8)$$

subject to the budget constraint,

$$\int_M^\infty F(z)c(z)\,dz - \int_M^R F(z)w(z)\,dz - F(M)a(M) = 0, \qquad (6.9)$$

where $a(M)$ is the amount of annuities at age M purchased from earlier savings:

$$a(M) = \frac{1}{F(M)}\int_0^M F(z)(w(z) - c(z))\,dz. \qquad (6.10)$$

Denote the solution to the maximization of (6.8) subject to (6.9) by $(\hat{c}(z), \hat{R})$. Of course, this solution depends on the level of $a(M)$, which is the instrument that is used by the self at age 0 to steer $(\hat{c}(z), \hat{R})$ in a desirable direction.

Note that V_M^1 is expected utility from the point of view of the age-M self. Expected utility beyond age M from the point of view of the age-0 self, denoted V_M^0, is

$$V_M^0 = \int_M^\infty F(z)u(\hat{c}(z))\,dz - \int_M^{\hat{R}} F(z)e(z)\,dz \qquad (6.11)$$

The optimum level of consumption up to age M is obtained by maximization of

$$V = \int_0^M F(z)u(c(z))\,dz - \int_0^M F(z)e(z)\,dz + V_M^0 \qquad (6.12)$$

subject to (6.10). As before, optimum consumption is constant, $\hat{c}$, $0 \leq z \leq M$, and the optimum level of transfers is $\hat{a}(M)$.

To clarify the issue, it will suffice to follow the example in section 6.3. Under these assumptions, consumption beyond age M is given by

$$\hat{c}(z) = \frac{\beta}{\alpha}\left[w(1 - e^{-\alpha(\hat{R}-M)}) + \alpha a(M)\right]e^{(\alpha-\beta)(z-M)}, \quad z \geq M, \qquad (6.13)$$

while $\hat{R}$ is determined by

$$\frac{w}{\hat{c}(\hat{R})} = e(\hat{R}). \tag{6.14}$$

The second-order condition, $w[\alpha - \beta(1 - e^{-\alpha(\hat{R}-M)})] + a(M) > 0$, is assumed to be satisfied. Since $\beta > \alpha$, consumption decreases with age. An increase in $a(M)$ increases consumption at all ages and decreases the retirement age. The optimum level, $\hat{a}(M)$, is chosen by maximizing (6.11) with respect to c and $a(M)$. As in section 6.3, it is not possible to determine whether, at the optimum, the chosen retirement age is higher or lower than the first-best retirement age. At relatively low retirement ages (relative to age M), consumption is "excessively" high and hence the marginal utility of postponing retirement is low, leading to earlier retirement than in the first-best case. In this case there is an inducement to decrease savings at early ages, leading to a lower $a(M)$, lower consumption, and a higher retirement age. The opposite holds if retirement is at a relatively old age relative to M, where consumption that is "too low" can be increased by a larger $a(M)$.

CHAPTER 7

Moral Hazard

7.1 INTRODUCTION

The holding of annuities may lead individuals to devote additional resources to life extension or, more generally, to increasing survival probabilities. We shall show that such actions by an individual in a competitive annuity market lead to inefficient resource allocation. Specifically, this behavior, which is called *moral hazard*, leads to overinvestment in raising survival probabilities. The reason for this inefficiency is that individuals disregard the effect of their actions on the equilibrium rate of return on annuities. The impact of individuals disregarding their actions on the terms of insurance contracts is common in insurance markets. Perhaps moral hazard plays a relatively small role in annuity markets, as Finkelstein and Poterba (2004) speculate, but it is important to understand the potential direction of its effect.

Following the discussion in chapter 6, assume that survival functions depend on a parameter α, $F(z, \alpha)$. A decrease in α increases survival probabilities at all ages: $\partial F(z, \alpha)/\partial \alpha \leq 0$. Individuals can affect the level of α by investing resources, whose level is denoted by $m(\alpha)$, such as medical care and healthy nutrition. Increasing survival requires additional resources, $m'(\alpha) < 0$, with increasing marginal costs, $m''(\alpha) > 0$.

7.2 COMPARISON OF FIRST BEST AND COMPETITIVE EQUILIBRIUM

Let us first examine the first-best allocation. With consumption constant at all ages, the resource constraint is now

$$c \int_0^T F(z, \alpha)\, dz - \int_0^R F(z, \alpha)\, w(z)\, dz + m(\alpha) = 0. \tag{7.1}$$

Maximizing expected utility, (4.1), with respect to c, R, and α yields the familiar first-order condition

$$u'(c)w(R) - e(R) = 0 \tag{7.2}$$

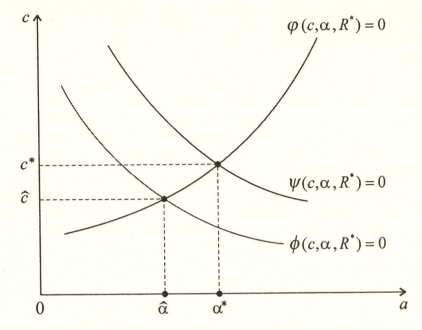

Figure 7.1. Investment in raising survival probabilities.

and the additional condition

$$(u(c) - u'(c)c) \int_0^T \frac{\partial F(z, \alpha)}{\partial \alpha} \, dz + \int_0^R \frac{\partial F(z, \alpha)}{\partial \alpha} (u(c)w(z)$$

$$- e(z)) \, dz - u'(c)m'(\alpha) = 0, \tag{7.3}$$

where, from (7.1),

$$c = c(R) = \frac{\int_0^R F(z, \alpha) \, w(z) \, dz - m(\alpha)}{\int_0^T F(z, \alpha) \, dz}. \tag{7.4}$$

Conditions (7.1)–(7.3) jointly determine the efficient allocation (c^*, R^*, α^*). Denote the left hand sides of (7.1) and (7.3) by $\varphi(c, \alpha, R)$ and $\psi(c, \alpha, R)$, respectively. We assume that second-order conditions are satisfied and relegate the technical analysis to the appendix. Figure 7.1 holds the optimum retirement age R^* constant and describes the conditions $\varphi(c, \alpha, R^*) = 0$ and $\psi(c, \alpha, R^*) = 0$.

Under competition, it is assumed that the level of expenditures on longevity, $m(\alpha)$, is *private information*. Hence, annuity-issuing firms cannot condition the rate of return on annuities on the level of these expenditures by annuitants. Let the rate of return faced by individuals at age z be $\tilde{r}(z)$. Then annuity holdings are given by

$$a(z) = \exp\left(\int_0^z \tilde{r}(x)\,dx\right)\left[\int_0^z \exp\left(-\int_0^x \tilde{r}(h)\,dh\right)(w(x) - c)\,dx - m(\alpha)\right],$$
$$(7.5)$$

and $a(T) = 0$, $w(z) = 0$ for $R \le z \le T$, yields the budget constraint

$$c\int_0^T \exp\left(-\int_0^z \tilde{R}(x)\,dx\right)dz - \int_0^R \exp\left(-\int_0^z \tilde{r}(x)\,dx\right)w(z)\,dz + m(\alpha) = 0.$$
$$(7.6)$$

Individuals maximize expected utility, (7.1), with respect to α, subject to (7.6):

$$u(c)\int_0^T \frac{\partial F(z, \alpha)}{\partial \alpha}\,dz - \int_0^R \frac{\partial F(z, \alpha)}{\partial \alpha}e(z)\,dz - u'(c)m'(\alpha) = 0. \qquad (7.7)$$

In competitive equilibrium, the no-arbitrage condition holds:

$$\tilde{r}(z) = -\frac{\partial \ln F(z, \alpha)}{\partial z}, \quad 0 \le z \le T. \qquad (7.8)$$

Condition (7.8) makes (7.6) equal to the resource constraint (7.1), and (7.7) can now be rewritten as

$$\phi(c, \alpha, R) = \psi(c, \alpha, R) + u'(c)\left(c\int_0^T \frac{\partial F(z, \alpha)}{\partial \alpha}\,dz\right.$$

$$\left. - \int_0^R \frac{\partial F(z, \alpha)}{\partial \alpha}w(z)\,dz\right) = 0. \qquad (7.9)$$

The condition with respect to the optimum R is seen to be (7.2). Denote the solutions to (7.1), (7.2), and (7.9) by $\hat{c}$, $\hat{\alpha}$, and $\hat{R}$., respectively. The last term in (7.9) is negative (see the appendix), so ϕ is placed relative to ψ as in figure 7.1 (holding R^* constant).

It is seen that $\hat{\alpha} < \alpha^*$ and $\hat{c} < c^*$. *Under competition, there is excessive investment in increasing survival probabilities and, consequently, consumption is lower.* The reason for the inefficiency, as already pointed out, is that individuals disregard the effect of their investments in α on the equilibrium rate of return on annuities.

It can be further inferred from condition (7.2) that optimum retirement age in a competitive equilibrium is higher than in the first-best allocation, $\hat{R} > R^*$ (consistent with excessive life lengthening under competition).

7.3 ANNUITY PRICES DEPENDING ON MEDICAL CARE

Fundamentally, the inefficiency of the competitive market is due to asymmetric information. If insurance firms and other issuers of annuities were able to monitor the resources devoted to life extension by individuals, $m(\alpha)$, and make the rate of return on annuities depend on its level (condition this return, say, on the medical plan that an individual has), then competition could attain the first best. With many suppliers of medical care and the multitude of factors affecting survival that are subject to individuals' decisions, symmetric information does not seem to be a reasonable assumption.

Appendix

$$\varphi(c, \alpha, R^*) = c \int_0^T F(z, \alpha)\, dz - \int_0^R F(z, \alpha) w(z)\, dz + m(\alpha) = 0 \quad (7A.1)$$

and

$$\psi(c, \alpha, R^*) = (u(c) - u'(c)c) \int_0^T \frac{\partial F(z, \alpha)}{\partial \alpha}\, dz$$

$$+ \int_0^{R^*} \frac{\partial F(z, \alpha)}{\partial \alpha} (u'(c)w - e(z))\, dz - u'(c) m'(\alpha) = 0. \quad (7A.2)$$

The first two terms in (7A.2) are the net marginal benefits in utility obtained from a marginal increase in survival probabilities, while the last term is the marginal cost of an increase in α. Indeed, concavity of $u(c)$ and condition (7.2) ensure that the first two terms in ψ are negative and the third is positive.

We assume that second-order conditions hold. Hence,

$$\frac{\partial \varphi}{\partial \alpha} = c \int_0^T \frac{\partial F(z, \alpha)}{\partial \alpha}\, dz - \int_0^{R^*} \frac{\partial F(z, \alpha)}{\partial \alpha} w(z)\, dz + m'(\alpha) < 0, \quad (7A.3)$$

from which it follows that

$$\frac{\partial \psi}{\partial \alpha} = -u''(c) \left(c \int_0^T \frac{\partial F(z, \alpha)}{\partial \alpha}\, dz - \int_0^{R^*} \frac{\partial F(z, \alpha)}{\partial \alpha} w(z)\, dz + m'(\alpha) \right) < 0.$$
$$(7A.4)$$

CHAPTER 8

Uncertain Future Survival Functions

8.1 FIRST BEST

So far we have assumed that all individuals have the same survival functions. We would now like to examine a heterogeneous population with respect to its survival functions.

A group of individuals who share a common survival function will be called a *risk class*. We shall consider a population that, at later stages in life, consists of a number of risk classes. Uncertainty about future risk-class realizations creates a demand by risk-averse individuals for insurance against this uncertainty. The goal of *disability benefits* programs, private or public, is to provide such insurance (usually, because of verification difficulties, only against extreme outcomes). Our goal is to examine whether annuities can provide such insurance.

In order to isolate the effects of heterogeneity in longevity from other differences among individuals, it is assumed that in all other respects—wages, utility of consumption, and disutility of labor—individuals are alike. Our goal is to analyze the first-best resource allocation and alternative competitive annuity pricing equilibria under heterogeneity in longevity.

It is difficult to predict early in life the relevant survival probabilities at later ages, as these depend on many factors (such as health and family circumstances) that unfold over time. For simplicity, we assume that up to a certain age, denoted M, well before the age of retirement, individuals have the same survival function, $F(z)$. At age M, there is a probability p, $0 < p < 1$, that the survival function becomes $F_1(z)$ (state of nature 1) and $1 - p$ that the survival function becomes $F_2(z)$ (state of nature 2). Survival probabilities are continuous and hence $F(M) = F_1(M) = F_2(M)$. It is assumed that $F_1(z)$ *stochastically dominates* $F_2(z)$ at all ages $M \leq z \leq T$.

Let $c(z)$ be consumption at age z, $0 \leq z \leq M$, and $c_i(z)$ be consumption at age z, $M \leq z \leq T$, of a risk-class-i (state-i) individual, $i = 1, 2$. Similarly, R_i is the age of retirement in state i, $i = 1, 2$.

An economy with a large number of individuals has a resource constraint that equates total expected wages to total expected consumption:

$$\int_0^M F(z)(w(z) - c(z))\,dz + p\left[\int_M^{R_1} F_1(z)w(z)\,dz - \int_M^T F_1(z)c_1(z)\,dz\right]$$

$$+(1-p)\left[\int_M^{R_2} F_2(z)w(z)\,dz - \int_M^T F_2(z)c_2(z)\,dz\right] = 0. \quad (8.1)$$

Expected lifetime utility is

$$V = \int_0^M F(z)u(c(z))\,dz + p\left[\int_M^T F_1(z)u(c_1(z))\,dz - \int_0^{R_1} F_1(z)e(z)\,dz\right]$$

$$+(1-p)\left[\int_M^T F_2(z)u(c_2(z))\,dz - \int_0^{R_2} F_2(z)e(z)\,dz\right]. \quad (8.2)$$

Denote the solution to the maximization of (8.2) subject to (8.1) by $(c^*(z),\ c_1^*(z),\ R_1^*,\ c_2^*(z),\ R_2^*)$. It can easily be shown that $c^*(z) = c_1^*(z) = c_2^*(z) = c^*$ for all $0 \le z \le T$ and that $R_1^* = R_2^* = R^*$. The solution $(c^*,\ R^*)$ satisfies

$$c^* = c^*(R^*) = \beta\frac{W_1(R^*)}{\bar{z}_1} + (1-\beta)\frac{W_2(R^*)}{\bar{z}_2}, \quad (8.3)$$

$$u'(c^*(R^*)w(R^*)) = e(R^*), \quad (8.4)$$

where $\bar{z}_i = \int_0^M F(z)\,dz + \int_M^T F_i(z)\,dz$ is life expectancy, $W_i(R) = \int_0^M F(z)w(z)\,dz + \int_M^R F_i(z)w(z)\,dz$ are expected wages until retirement in state i, $i = 1, 2$, and

$$\beta = \frac{p\bar{z}_1}{p\bar{z}_1 + (1-p)\bar{z}_2}, \quad 0 \le \beta \le 1.$$

This is an important result: *In the first best, optimum consumption and age of retirement are independent of the state of nature.*

This is equivalent, as we shall demonstrate, to *full insurance* against longevity risk and against risk-class classification. When information on longevity (survival functions) is unknown early in life, individuals have an interest in insuring themselves against alternative risk-class classifications, and the first-best solution reflects such (ex ante) insurance.

Importantly, the first-best allocation, (8.3) and (8.4), involves transfers across states of nature. Let S denote expected savings up to age M, defined as the difference between expected wages and optimum consumption:

$$S = \int_0^M F(z)(w(z) - c^*)\, dz. \tag{8.5}$$

Define *optimum transfers* to risk class i, denoted T_i^*, as the excess of expected consumption over expected wages from age M to T less expected savings during ages 0 to M:

$$T_i^* = c^* \int_M^T F_i(z)\, dz - \int_M^{R^*} F(z)w(z)\, dz - S = c^* \bar{z}_i + W_i(R^*). \tag{8.6}$$

By (8.6),

$$T_1^* = \bar{z}_1 (1 - \beta) \left[\frac{W_2(R^*)}{\bar{z}_2} - \frac{W_1(R^*)}{\bar{z}_1} \right],$$

$$T_2^* = \bar{z}_2 \beta \left[\frac{W_1(R^*)}{\bar{z}_1} - \frac{W_2(R^*)}{\bar{z}_2} \right]. \tag{8.7}$$

We have assumed that wages, $w(z)$, are nonincreasing with z.[1] Under this assumption transfers to the stochastically dominant group with higher life expectancy are positive, $T_1^* > 0$, and transfers to the dominated group with shorter life expectancy are negative, $T_2^* < 0$.

Since $F_1(z)$ stochastically dominates $F_2(z)$,

$$\frac{W_2(R^*)}{\bar{z}_2} - \frac{W_1(R^*)}{\bar{z}_1} \geq w(z_c)$$

$$\times \left[\frac{\int_0^M F(z)\, dz + \int_M^{R^*} F_2(z)\, dz}{\bar{z}_2} - \frac{\int_0^M F(z) + \int_M^{R^*} F_1(z)\, dz \bar{z}_1}{F} \right]$$

$$> \left[\frac{\int_0^M F(z)\, dz + \int_M^T F_2(z)\, dz}{\bar{z}_2} - \frac{\int_0^M F(z) + \int_M^T F_1(z)\, dz}{\bar{z}_1} \right] = 0, \tag{8.8}$$

where z_c is the age at which the two functions $F_i(z)/\bar{z}_i$, $i = 1, 2$, intersect. The resource constraint (8.1) means that total expected transfers are 0: $pT_1^* + (1 - p)T_2^* = 0$.

---

[1] Recall that $w'(z) \leq 0$, $0 \leq z \leq T$, is a sufficient condition for the unique determination of optimum consumption and retirement.

8.2 Competitive Separating Equilibrium (Risk-class Pricing)

Consider a competitive market in which individuals who purchase or sell annuities are identified by their risk classes. Identification is either exogenous or due to actions of individuals that reveal their risk classes.[2] As above, during ages 0 to M, all individuals are assumed to belong to the same risk class. At ages beyond M, individuals belong either to risk class 1 or to risk class 2 and, accordingly, their trading of annuities is at the respective risk-class returns.

Whether a competitive annuity market can or cannot attain the first-best allocation depends on the *terms of the annuities' payouts*. We distinguish between short-term and long-term annuities. A *short-term annuity* pays an instantaneous return and is redeemed for cash by a surviving holder of the annuity.[3] A *long-term annuity* pays a flow of returns, specified in advance, over a certain period of time or indefinitely. When the short-run returns of annuities' depend only on age according to a known survival function, the purchase or sale of a long-term annuity is equivalent to a sequence of purchases or sales of short-term annuities. However, upon the arrival of information on and the differentiation between risk classes, this equivalence disappears. Once information on an individual's risk class is revealed, the terms of newly purchased or sold annuities become risk-class-specific. The no-arbitrage condition, which is equivalent to zero expected profits, now applies separately to each risk class. On the other hand, long-term annuities purchased prior to the arrival of risk-class information yield a predetermined flow of returns which, in equilibrium, reflect the *expected* relative weight of different risk classes in the population.

Because of their predetermined terms, long-term annuities provide, insurance against risk-class classification. This will be demonstrated to be crucial for the efficiency of competitive annuity markets.

We shall first show that if annuities are only short-term, then a competitive annuity market cannot attain the first best. Subsequently we shall demonstrate that the availability of long-term annuities enables the competitive annuity market to attain the first best.

---

[2] This is further discussed in chapter 9.

[3] In practice, of course, "instantaneous" typically means "annual," that is, a 1-year annuity.

8.3 Equilibrium with Short-term Annuities

During the first phase of life, individuals have the same survival functions and the purchase or sale of annuities is governed by

$$\dot{a}(z) = r(z)a(z) + w(z) - c(z), \quad 0 \le z \le M, \tag{8.9}$$

or, since $a(0) = 0$,

$$a(z) = \exp\left(\int_0^z r(x)\,dx\right)\left[\int_0^z \exp\left(-\int_0^x r(h)\,dh\right)(w(x) - c(x))\,dx\right],$$

$$0 \le z \le M. \tag{8.10}$$

Applying the no-arbitrage condition, $r(z) = f(z)/F(z)$, (8.10) can be rewritten as

$$F(M)a(M) = \int_0^M F(z)(w(z) - c(z))\,dz. \tag{8.11}$$

Maximization of expected utility for $0 \le z \le M$ yields constant consumption, denoted c, whose level depends, of course, on the expected level of annuities held at age M, $F(M)a(M)$. This level of annuities, (8.11), is equal to expected total savings up to age M.

Since all annuities are short-term, the stock $a(M)$ is converted into new annuities by individuals alive at age M. The dynamics after age M are governed by the relevant risk-class rate of return. Consider an individual who belongs to risk class i, $i = 1, 2$. Denote the annuities held by this individual by $a_i(z)$. The purchase and sale of annuities are governed by

$$\dot{a}_i(z) = r_i(z)a_i(z) + w(z) - c_i(z), \quad M \le z \le T, \tag{8.12}$$

or

$$a_i(z) = \exp\left(\int_M^z r_i(x)\,dx\right)\left[\int_M^z \exp\left(-\int_M^z r_i(h)\,dh\right)\right.$$

$$\left. \times (w(x) - c_i(x))\,dx + a(M)\right], \quad M \le z \le T, \tag{8.13}$$

where $r_i(z)$ is the rate of return on annuities held by risk-class-i individuals. At age M the individual holds $a_i(M) = a(M)$, having converted savings into risk-class-i annuities. The no arbitrage condition applies to each risk class separately, $r_i = f_i(z)/F_i(z)$, $i = 1, 2$. Taking, in

(8.13), $z = T$ and $a_i(T) = 0$, we obtain

$$\int_M^T F_i(z)(w(z) - c_i(z))\, dz + F(M)a(M) = 0. \tag{8.14}$$

Maximization of expected utility for $M \leq z \leq T$, conditional on being in state i, yields constant optimum consumption, denoted c_i. From (8.11) and (8.14), c and c_i are related by the condition

$$\int_0^M F(z)(w(z) - c)\, dz + \int_M^T F_i(z)(w(z) - c_i) = 0, \quad i = 1, 2 \tag{8.15}$$

(with $w(z) = 0$ for $R_i \leq z \leq T$). Maximization of expected utility, (8.2), with respect to c, taking into account relation (8.15), yields

$$u'(\hat{c}) = pu'(\hat{c}_1) + (1 - p)u'(\hat{c}_2). \tag{8.16}$$

Optimum consumption during early ages, $0 \leq z \leq M$, is a weighted average of optimum consumption of the two risk classes after age M.[4] Rewriting (8.15),

$$\hat{c}_i = \frac{W_i(R_i) - \hat{c}\int_0^M F(z)\, dz}{\int_M^T F_i(z)\, dz}, \quad i = 1, 2. \tag{8.17}$$

Equations (8.16) and (8.17) determine the optimum $\hat{c}$ and $\hat{c}_i$, $i = 1, 2$.

Optimum retirement age in state i, $\hat{R}_i$, is determined by the familiar condition

$$u'(\hat{c}_i)w(\hat{R}_i) = e(\hat{R}_i), \quad i = 1, 2. \tag{8.18}$$

Can the solution to (8.16)–(8.18) be the first-best allocation? To see that this is not possible, suppose that $c^* = \hat{c} = \hat{c}_1 = \hat{c}_2$ and $\hat{R}_1 = \hat{R}_2 = R^*$. Then (8.17) implies that $W_1(R^*)/\bar{z}_1 = W_2(R^*)/\bar{z}_2$. It has been assumed, however, that $F_1(z)$ stochastically dominates $F_2(z)$, and therefore, as shown above, $W_1(R^*)/\bar{z}_1 < W_2(R^*)/\bar{z}_2$. This proves that the first-best solution is impossible.

Specifically, stochastic dominance of $F_1(z)$ over $F_2(z)$ implies that $\hat{c}_1 < \hat{c} < \hat{c}_2$ for any given R. Hence, by (8.18), $\hat{R}_1 > \hat{R}_2$ (figure 8.1).

We summarize: *When there are only short-term annuities, a separating competitive equilibrium is not first best. Competitive equilibrium leads to consumption and retirement ages that differ by risk class.*

---

[4] The optimum amount of annuities at age M, $\dfrac{1}{F(M)}\displaystyle\int_0^M F(z)(w(z) - \hat{c})\, dz$, may be negative, which means that a surviving individual undertakes at age M a contingent debt equal to this amount.

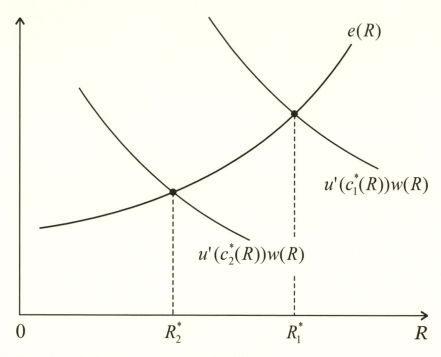

Figure 8.1. Optimum retirement ages by risk class.

The reason for this result is straightforward: The first best requires insurance against risk-class classification that entails transfers across states of nature. These transfers cannot be implemented with short-term annuities. We shall now demonstrate that with long-term annuities the competitive equilibrium is first best.

8.4 The Efficiency of Equilibrium with Long-term Annuities

Suppose that annuities can be held by individuals for any length of time and that their future stream of returns is fully specified at the time of purchase or sale. We continue to denote the annuities held by individuals during their early ages by $a(z)$, $0 \leq z \leq M$. The rate of return on these annuities at age z is denoted, as before, by $r(z)$. Competitive trading in these annuities satisfies the no-arbitrage condition, $r(z) = f(z)/F(z)$, $0 < z \leq M$.

Under full information about the identity of annuity purchasers and sellers, trades in annuities by individuals older than M are performed at risk-class-specific rates of return. Thus, an individual of age $z > M$

who belongs to risk class i, trades annuities at the rate of return $r_i(z) = f_i(z)/F_i(z)$, $i = 1, 2$. After age M, the stock of long-term annuities held at age M, $a(M)$, continues to provide, contingent on survival, a *predetermined* flow of returns, $r(z)$. The individual may sell (when $a(M) > 0$) or repay a contingent debt (when $a(M) < 0$) at risk-class-specific prices that reflect the expected returns of these annuities *to this individual*, $a(M) \int_M^T F_i(z) r(z) \, dz$.

The dynamics of the individual's budget up to age M are the same as in (8.7), and hence (8.11) holds. With constant optimum consumption, c,

$$F(M)a(M) = \int_0^M F(z)(w(z) - c) \, dz. \tag{8.19}$$

The purchase or sale of annuities by a risk-class-i individual is governed by

$$\dot{a}_i(z) = r_i(z)a_i(z) + w(z) - c_i(z) + r(z)a(M), \quad M \le z \le T, \quad i = 1, 2, \tag{8.20}$$

where $r_i(z) = f_i(z)/F_i(z)$ and $a_i(M) = 0$. Multiplying both sides of (8.20) by $F_i(z)$ and integrating by parts, we obtain

$$\int_M^T F_i(z)(w(z) - c_i) \, dz + a(M) \int_M^T F_i(z) r(z) \, dz = 0, \quad i = 1, 2, \tag{8.21}$$

or, by (8.19),

$$\int_M^T F_i(z)(w(z) - c_i) \, dz - \frac{1}{F(M)} \int_0^M F(z)(w(z) - c) \, dz \int_M^T F_i(z) r(z) \, dz = 0 \tag{8.22}$$

(with $w(z) = 0$ for $R_i \le z \le T$). The optimum age of retirement in state i, R_i^*, is determined by

$$u'(c_i)w(R_i^*) = e(R_i^*), \quad i = 1, 2. \tag{8.23}$$

Multiplying (8.22) by p for $i = 1$ and by $1 - p$ for $i = 2$, and adding, we obtain

$$p \int_M^T F_1(z)(w(z) - c_1) \, dz + (1 - p) \int_M^T F_2(z)(w(z) - c_2) \, dz$$

$$= \frac{1}{F(M)} \int_0^M F(z)(w(z) - c) \, dz \int_M^T (pF_1(z) + (1 - p)F_2(z))r(z) \, dz = 0. \tag{8.24}$$

Now let

$$r(z) = \frac{pF_1(z)r_1(z) + (1 - p)F_2(z)r_2(z)}{pF_1(z) + (1 - p)F_2(z)}$$

$$= \delta r_1(z) + (1 - \delta)r_2(z), \quad M \le z \le T, \tag{8.25}$$

where

$$\delta = \delta(z) = \frac{pF_1(z)}{pF_1(z) + (1 - p)F_2(z)}, \quad 0 < \delta(z) < 1. \tag{8.26}$$

The future instantaneous rate of return at any age $z \ge M$ on long-term annuities held at age M is a weighted average of the risk-class rates of return, the weights being the fraction of each risk class in the population.[5] Inserting (8.25) into (8.24), the latter becomes

$$p\int_M^T F_1(z)(w(z) - c_1)\, dz + (1 - p)\int_M^T F_2(z)(w(z) - c_2)\, dz$$

$$+ \int_0^M F(z)(w(z) - c)\, dz = 0. \tag{8.27}$$

From (8.27) it is now straightforward to draw the following conclusion: *The unique solution to (8.22) and (8.23) that satisfies (8.1), with $r(z)$ given by (8.25), is $c = c_1 = c_2 = c^*$ and $R_1^* = R_2^* = R^*$, where (c^*, R^*) is the First-Best solution (8.3) and (8.4).*

A separating competitive equilibrium with long-term annuities supports the first-best allocation. Individuals are able to insure themselves against uncertainty with respect to their future risk class by purchasing long-term annuities early in life. In equilibrium these annuities yield at every age a rate of return equal to the population average of risk class rates of return. The returns from these annuities provide an individual with a consumption level that is independent of risk-class realization.

The transfers across states of nature necessary for the first-best allocation are obtained through the *revaluation of long-term annuities.* The stochastically dominant risk class obtains a windfall because the annuities held by individuals in this class are worth more because of the

---

[5] The change in $r(z)$ is $\dot{r}(z) = \left(\dfrac{\delta r_1}{\delta r_1 + (1 - \delta)r_2}\right)\dfrac{f_1'(z)}{f_1(z)} + \left(\dfrac{(1 - \delta)r_2}{\delta r_1 + (1 - \delta)r_2}\right)\dfrac{f_2'(z)}{f_2(z)}.$
The sign of this expression can be negative or positive. The change in the hazard rate, $\dfrac{f(z)}{F(z)}$, is equal to $\dfrac{f(z)}{F(z)}\left(\dfrac{f'(z)}{f(z)} + \dfrac{f(z)}{F(z)}\right)$. A nondecreasing hazard rate implies that $-\dfrac{f'(z)}{f(z)} \le \dfrac{f(z)}{F(z)}$ but does not sign $\dfrac{f'(z)}{f(z)}$ (for the exponential function, $f'(z) < 0$, and this inequality becomes an equality).

higher life expectancy of the owners. The other risk class experiences a loss for the opposite reason.

Another important implication of the fact that in equilibrium consumption is independent of the state of nature is the following. From (8.20) it is seen that when $c_i = c^*$, $i = 1, 2$, the solution to (8.20) has $\dot{a}_i(z) = a_i(z) = 0$, $M \leq z \leq T$. Thus: *The market for risk class annuities after age M (sometimes called "the residual market") is inactive. Under full information, the competitive equilibrium yields zero trading in annuities after age M.* As argued above and seen from (8.21), the interpretation of this result is that the flow of returns from annuities held at age M can be matched, using the relevant risk-class survival function of the holder of the annuities, to finance a constant flow of consumption:

$$c^* = \frac{\int_M^{R^*} F_i(z)w(z)\,dz + a^*(M)\int_M^T F_i(z)r(z)\,dz}{\int_M^T F_i(z)\,dz}, \qquad (8.28)$$

where $a^*(M)$ is the optimum level of annuities at age M:

$$a^*(M) = \frac{1}{F(M)}\int_0^M F(z)(w(z) - c^*)\,dz.$$

8.5 Example: Exponential Survival Functions

Let $F(z) = e^{-\alpha z}$, $0 \leq z \leq M$, and $F_i(z) = e^{-\alpha M}e^{-\alpha_i(z-M)}$, $M \leq z \leq \infty$, $i = 1, 2$. Assume further that wages are constant; $w(z) = w$.

With a constant level of consumption, c, before age M, the level of annuities held at age M is

$$a(M) = \frac{1}{F(M)}\int_0^M F(z)(w - c)\,dz = \left(\frac{w - c}{\alpha}\right)\left(e^{\alpha M} - 1\right).$$

For the above survival function, the risk-class rates of return at age $z \geq M$ are α_i, $i = 1, 2$. We assume that risk class 1 stochastically dominates risk class 2, $\alpha_1 < \alpha_2$. Annuities yield a rate of return, $r(z)$, that is a weighted average of these returns: $r(z) = \delta(z)\alpha_1 + (1 - \delta(z))\alpha_2$, where

$$\delta(z) = \frac{pe^{-\alpha_1(z-M)}}{pe^{-\alpha_1(z-M)} + (1 - p)e^{-\alpha_2(z-M)}}. \qquad (8.29)$$

The weight $\delta(z)$ is the fraction of risk class 1 in the population. It increases from p to 1 as z increases from M to ∞. Accordingly, $r(z)$ decreases with z from $p\alpha_1 + (1 - p)\alpha_2$ at $z = M$, approaching α_1 as $z \to \infty$ (figure 8.2).

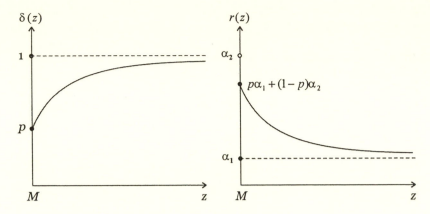

Figure 8.2. The rate of return on long-term annuities.

Consumption after age M for a risk-class-i individual is constant, c_i, and the budget constraint is $w\int_M^R F_i(z)\,dz - c_i\int_M^T F_i(z) + a_M\int_M^T F_i(z)r(z)\,dz = 0$. For our case it is equal to

$$\frac{we^{-\alpha M}}{\alpha_i}\left(1 - e^{-\alpha_i(R_i-M)}\right) - \frac{c_i}{\alpha_i}e^{-\alpha M}$$

$$+\left(\frac{w-c}{\alpha}\right)\left(1 - e^{-\alpha M}\right)\int_M^T e^{-\alpha_i(z-M)}r(z)\,dz = 0, \quad i = 1, 2. \tag{8.30}$$

Multiplying (8.13) by p for $i = 1$ and by $1 - p$ for $i = 2$, and adding, it can be seen that the unique solution to (8.30) is $c^* = c_1 = c_2$ and $R^* = R_1 = R_2$, where

$$c^* = \frac{w\left[\dfrac{1}{\alpha}(e^{\alpha M} - 1) + \dfrac{p}{\alpha_1}(1 - e^{-\alpha_1(R^*-M)}) + \dfrac{1-p}{\alpha_2}(1 - e^{-\alpha_2(R^*-M)})\right]}{\dfrac{1}{\alpha}(e^{\alpha M} - 1) + \dfrac{p}{\alpha_1} + \dfrac{1-p}{\alpha_2}}. \tag{8.31}$$

CHAPTER 9

Pooling Equilibrium and Adverse Selection

9.1 INTRODUCTION

For a competitive annuity market with long-term annuities to be efficient, it must be assumed that individuals can be identified by their risk classes. We now wish to explore the existence of an equilibrium in which the individuals' risk classes are unknown and cannot be revealed by their actions. This is called a *pooling equilibrium.*

Annuities are offered in a pooling equilibrium at the same price to all individuals (assuming that nonlinear prices, which require exclusivity, as in Rothschild and Stiglitz (1979), are not feasible). Consequently, the equilibrium price of annuities is equal to the average longevity of the annuitants, *weighted by the equilibrium amounts purchased by different risk classes*. This result has two important implications. One, the amount of annuities purchased by individuals with high longevity is larger than in a separating, efficient equilibrium, and the opposite holds for individuals with low longevities. This is termed *adverse selection*. Two, adverse selection causes the prices of annuities to exceed the present values of expected average actuarial payouts.

The empirical importance of adverse selection is widely debated (see, for example, Chiapori and Salanie (2000), though its presence is visible. For example, from the data in Brown et al. (2001), one can derive survival rates for males and females born in 1935, distinguishing between the overall population average rates and the rates applicable to annuitants, that is, those who purchase private annuities. As figures 9.1(a) and (b) clearly display, at all ages annuitants, whether males or females, have higher survival rates than the population average rates (table 9A.1 in the appendix provides the underlying data). Adverse selection seems somewhat smaller among females, perhaps because of the smaller variance in female survival rates across different occupations and educational groups.

Adverse selection may be reflected not only in the *amounts* of annuities purchased by different risk classes but also in the *selection of different insurance instruments*, such as different types of annuities. We explore this important issue in chapter 11.

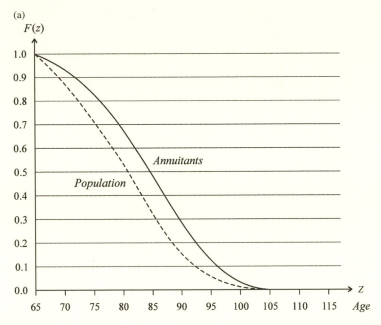

Figure 9.1(a). Male survival functions (1935 cohort). (*Source*: Brown et al. 2001, table 1.1).

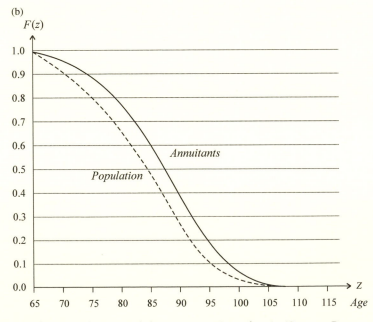

Figure 9.1(b). Female survival functions (1935 cohort). (*Source*: Brown et al. 2001, table 1.1).

9.2 GENERAL MODEL

We continue to denote the flow of returns on long-term annuities purchased prior to age M by $r(z)$, $M \leq z \leq T$.

The dynamic budget constraint of a risk-class-i individual, $i = 1, 2$, is now

$$\dot{a}_i(z) = r_p(z)a_i(z) + w(z) - c_i(z) + r(z)a(M), \quad M \leq z \leq T, \quad (9.1)$$

where $\dot{a}_i(z)$ are annuities purchased or sold (with $a_i(M) = 0$) and $r_p(z)$ is the rate of return in the (pooled) annuity market for age-z individuals, $M \leq z \leq T$.

For any consumption path, the demand for annuities is, by (9.1),

$$a_i(z) = \exp\left(\int_M^z r_p(x)\,dx\right)\left[\int_M^z \exp\left(-\int_M^x r_p(h)\,dh\right)\right.$$

$$\left. \times (w(x) - c_i(x) + r(x)a(M))\,dx\right], \quad i = 1, 2. \quad (9.2)$$

Maximization of expected utility,

$$\int_M^T F_i(z)u(c_i(z))\,dz, \quad i = 1, 2, \quad (9.3)$$

subject to (9.1) yields optimum consumption, denoted $\hat{c}_i(z)$,

$$\hat{c}_i(z) = \hat{c}_i(M)\exp\left(\int_M^z \frac{1}{\sigma}(r_p(x) - r_i(x))\,dx\right), \quad M \leq z \leq T, \quad i = 1, 2 \quad (9.4)$$

(where σ is evaluated at $\hat{c}_i(x)$). It is seen that $\hat{c}_i(z)$ increases or decreases with age depending on the sign of $r_p(z) - r_i(z)$. Optimum consumption at age M, $c_i(M)$, is found from (9.2), setting $a_i(T) = 0$,

$$\int_M^T \exp\left(-\int_M^x r_p(h)\,dh\right)(w(x) - \hat{c}_i(x) + r(x)a(M))\,dx = 0, \quad i = 1, 2. \quad (9.5)$$

Substituting for $\hat{c}_i(x)$, from (9.4),

$$\hat{c}_i(M) = \frac{\int_M^T \exp\left(-\int_M^x r_p(h)\,dh\right)(w(x) + r(x)a(M))\,dx}{\int_M^T \exp\left(\int_M^x \frac{1}{\sigma}((1 - \sigma)r_p(h) - r_i(h))\,dh\right)dx}, \quad i = 1, 2. \quad (9.6)$$

Since $r_1(z) < r_2(z)$ for all z, $M \leq z \leq T$, it follows from (9.6) that $\hat{c}_1(M) < \hat{c}_2(M)$. Inserting optimum consumption $\hat{c}_i(x)$ into (9.2), we obtain the optimum demand for annuities, $\hat{a}_i(z)$.

Since $\hat{a}_i(M) = 0$, it is seen from (9.1) that $\dot{\hat{a}}_1(M) > \dot{\hat{a}}_2(M)$. In fact, it can be shown (see appendix) that $\hat{a}_1(z) > \hat{a}_2(z)$ for all $M < z < T$.

This is to be expected: *At all ages, the stochastically dominant risk class, having higher longevity, holds more annuities compared to the risk class with lower longevity.*

We wish to examine whether there exists an equilibrium pooling rate of return, $r_p(z)$, that satisfies the aggregate resource constraint (zero expected profits). Multiplying (9.1) by $F_i(z)$ and integrating by parts, we obtain

$$\int_M^T F_i(z)(r_p(z) - r_i(z))\hat{a}_i(z)\, dz$$

$$= \int_M^T F_i(z)(w(z) - \hat{c}_i(z))dz + a_M \int_M^T r(z)\, dz, \quad i = 1, 2. \qquad (9.7)$$

Multiplying (9.7) by p for $i = 1$ and by $(1 - p)$ for $i = 2$, and adding,

$$\int_M^T [(pF_1(z)\hat{a}_1(z) + (1 - p)F_2(z)\hat{a}_2(z))\, r_p(z)$$

$$- (pF_1(z)\hat{a}_1(z)r_1(z) + (1 - p)F_2(z)\hat{a}_2(z)r_2(z))]\, dz$$

$$= p \int_M^T F_1(z)(w(z) - \hat{c}_1(z))\, dz + (1 - p) \int_T^M F_2(z)(w(z) - \hat{c}_2(z))\, dz$$

$$+ a(M) \int_M^T (pF_1(z) + (1 - p)F_2(z))\, r(z)\, dz. \qquad (9.8)$$

Recall that

$$r(z) = \frac{pF_1(z)r_1(z) + (1 - p)F_2(z)r_2(z)}{pF_1(z) + (1 - p)F_2(z)}$$

is the rate of return on annuities purchased prior to age M. Hence the last term on the right hand side of (9.8) is equal to $F(M)a(M) = \int_0^M F(z)(w(z) - c)\, dz$. Thus, the no-arbitrage condition in the pooled market is satisfied if and only if the left hand side of (9.8) is equal to 0 for all z:

$$r_p(z) = \gamma(z)r_1(z) + (1 - \gamma(z))r_2(z), \tag{9.9}$$

where

$$\gamma(z) = \frac{pF_1(z)\hat{a}_1(z)}{pF_1(z)\hat{a}_1(z) + (1 - p)\hat{a}_2(z)}. \tag{9.10}$$

The equilibrium pooling rate of return takes into account the amount of annuities purchased or sold by the two risk classes. Assuming that $\hat{a}_i(z) > 0$, $i = 1, 2$, $r_p(z)$ is seen to be a weighted average of $r_1(z)$ and $r_2(z)$: $r_1(z) < r_p(z) < r_2(z)$. In the appendix we discuss the conditions that ensure positive holdings of annuities by both risk classes.

Comparing (9.9) and (9.10) with (8.25) and (8.26), it is seen that $r_p(z) < r(z)$ for all z, $M < z < T$. *The pooling rate of return on annuities, reflecting adverse selection in the purchase of annuities in equilibrium, is lower than the rate of return on annuities purchased prior to the realization of different risk classes.*

Indeed, as described in the introduction to this chapter, Brown et al. (2001) compared mortality tables for annuitants to those for the general population for both males and females and found significantly higher expected lifetimes for the former.

In chapter 11 we shall explore another aspect of adverse selection, annuitants' self-selection leading to sorting among *different types of annuities* according to equilibrium prices.

9.3 EXAMPLE

Assume that $u(c) = \ln c$, $F(z) = e^{-\alpha z}$, $0 \leq z \leq M$, $F_i(z) = e^{-\alpha M}e^{-\alpha_i(z-M)}$, $M \leq z \leq \infty$, $i = 1, 2$, $w(z) = w$ constant and let retirement age, R, be independent of risk class.[1] Under these assumptions, (9.6) becomes

$$\hat{c}_i(M) = \alpha_i \int_M^\infty \exp\left(-\int_M^x r_p(h)\, dh\right)(w(x) + r(x)a(M))\, dx, \tag{9.11}$$

where $w(x) = w$ for $M \leq x \leq R$ and $w(x) = 0$ for $x > R$.

---

[1] Individuals have an inelastic infinite labor disutility at R and zero disutility at ages $z < R$.

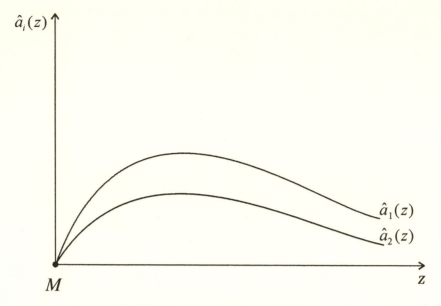

Figure 9.2. Demand for annuities in a pooling equilibrium.

Demand for annuities, (9.2), is now

$$\hat{a}_i(z) = \exp\left(\int_M^z r_p(x)\,dx\right)\int_M^x \exp\left(-\int_M^x r_p(h)\,dh\right)(w(x)+r(x)a(M))\,dx$$

$$-\left(1-e^{-\alpha_i(z-M)}\right)\int_M^\infty \exp\left(-\int_M^x r_p(h)\,dh\right)(w(x)+r(x)a(M))\,dx.$$

$$(9.12)$$

Clearly, $a_i(M) = a_i(\infty) = 0$, $i = 1, 2$, and since $\alpha_1 < \alpha_2$, it follows that $\hat{a}_1(z) > \hat{a}_2(z)$ for all $z > M$. From (9.1),

$$\dot{\hat{a}}_i(M) = w\left(1 - \alpha_i\int_M^R \exp\left(-\int_M^x r_p(h)\,dh\right)dx\right) + a(M)$$

$$\times\left(r(M) - \alpha_i\int_M^\infty \exp\left(-\int_M^x r_p(h)\,dh\right)r(x)\,dx\right), \quad i = 1, 2.$$

$$(9.13)$$

Since $r(x)$ decreases in x, (8.29), it is seen that if $r_p(x) > \alpha_1$, then for $i = 1$, both terms in (9.13) are positive, and hence $\dot{\hat{a}}_1(M) > 0$. From (9.12) it can then be inferred that $\hat{a}_1(z) > 0$ with the shape in figure 9.2.

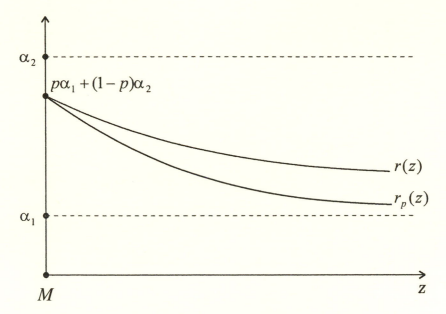

Figure 9.3. Return on annuities in a pooling equilibrium.

Additional conditions are required to ensure that $\dot{a}_2(M) > 0$, from which it follows that $\hat{a}_2(z) > 0$, $z \geq M$. Thus, the existence of a pooling equilibrium depends on parameter configuration. When $\hat{a}_2(z) > 0$ (figure 9.2), then $r(z) = \delta(z)\alpha_1 + (1-\delta)\alpha_2 > r_p(z) = \gamma(z)\alpha_1 + (1-\gamma(z))\alpha_2$ because when $\hat{a}_1(z) > \hat{a}_2(z)$, then (figure 9.3)

$$\delta(z) = \frac{pe^{-\alpha_1(z-M)}}{pe^{-\alpha_1(z-M)} + (1-p)e^{-\alpha_2(z-M)}}$$

$$> \frac{pe^{-\alpha_1(z-M)}\hat{a}_1(z)}{pe^{-\alpha_1(z-M)}\hat{a}_1(z) + (1-p)e^{-\alpha_2(z-M)}\hat{a}_2(z)} = \gamma(z).$$

What remains to be determined is the optimum $\hat{a}(M)$, $\hat{a}(M) = ((w - \hat{c})/\alpha)(e^{\alpha M} - 1)$, or, equivalently, consumption prior to age M, $\hat{c} = w - \alpha\hat{a}(M)/(e^{\alpha M} - 1)$. By (9.11), $\hat{c}_i(M)$, $i = 1, 2$, depend directly on $\hat{a}(M)$. Maximizing expected utility (disregarding labor disutility),

$$V = \int_0^M e^{-\alpha z} \ln c \, dz + pe^{-\alpha M} \int_M^\infty e^{-\alpha_1(z-M)} \ln \hat{c}_1(z) \, dz$$

$$+ (1 - p)e^{-\alpha M} \int_M^\infty e^{-\alpha_2(z-M)} \ln \hat{c}_2(z) \, dz, \qquad (9.14)$$

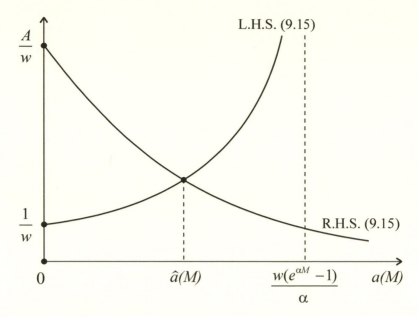

Figure 9.4. Amount of long-term annuities purchased early in life:
$\left(A = \int_M^\infty \exp\left(-\int_M^x r_p(h)\,dh\right) r(x)\,dx / \int_M^R \exp\left(-\int_M^x r_p(h)\,dh\right) dx > 1 \right)$.

with respect to $a(M)$, using (9.11), yields the first-order condition for an interior solution that can be written, after some manipulations as

$$\frac{e^{\alpha M} - 1}{w(e^{\alpha M} - 1) - \alpha a(M)} = \left(\frac{p}{\alpha_1} + \frac{p}{\alpha_2}\right)$$

$$\times \left(\frac{\int_M^\infty \exp(-\int_M^x r_p(h)\,dh) r(x)\,dx}{\int_M^\infty \exp\left(-\int_M^x r_p(h)\,dh\right)(w(x) + c(x)a(M))\,dx} \right)$$

$$(9.15)$$

The left-hand side of (9.15) increases with $a(M)$, while the right hand side decreases with $a(M)$ (figure 9.4).

Appendix

A. Survival Rates for a 1935 Birth Cohort

TABLE 9.A.1.

Age	Population		Annuitants	
	Male	Female	Male	Female
65	0.978503	0.986735	0.989007	0.992983
66	0.955567	0.972336	0.977086	0.985266
67	0.931401	0.956873	0.964103	0.976922
68	0.906303	0.940484	0.949935	0.967886
69	0.880455	0.923244	0.934490	0.958116
70	0.853800	0.905086	0.917697	0.947530
71	0.826172	0.885875	0.899490	0.936004
72	0.797493	0.865541	0.879829	0.923386
73	0.767666	0.843998	0.858678	0.909496
74	0.736589	0.821157	0.835989	0.894166
75	0.704187	0.796868	0.811695	0.877234
76	0.670393	0.771044	0.785733	0.858575
77	0.635149	0.743735	0.758039	0.838109
78	0.598456	0.715046	0.728578	0.815799
79	0.560408	0.685027	0.697360	0.791601
80	0.521200	0.653585	0.664443	0.765431
81	0.481108	0.620632	0.629934	0.737205
82	0.440451	0.586205	0.593975	0.706870
83	0.399581	0.550354	0.556727	0.674371
84	0.358884	0.513134	0.518386	0.639648
85	0.318805	0.474641	0.479222	0.602670
86	0.279836	0.435065	0.439561	0.563491
87	0.242486	0.394715	0.399797	0.522278
88	0.207251	0.354020	0.360364	0.479344
89	0.174563	0.313509	0.321725	0.435214
90	0.144767	0.273776	0.284338	0.390583
91	0.118099	0.235444	0.248635	0.346256
92	0.094678	0.199121	0.214996	0.302021
93	0.074510	0.165364	0.183735	0.260889
94	0.057496	0.134641	0.155093	0.222355
95	0.043497	0.107438	0.129260	0.187020
96	0.032263	0.084018	0.106332	0.155292
97	0.023472	0.064413	0.086313	0.127382
98	0.016760	0.048453	0.069084	0.103228
99	0.011757	0.035806	0.054455	0.082603
100	0.008094	0.025961	0.042188	0.065170
101	0.005462	0.018442	0.032040	0.050582
102	0.003608	0.012814	0.023776	0.038510
103	0.002329	0.008695	0.017172	0.028653
104	0.001467	0.005751	0.012013	0.020738

TABLE 9.A.1.
Continued.

| Age | Population | | Annuitants | |
	Male	Female	Male	Female
105	0.000901	0.003699	0.008094	0.014519
106	0.000538	0.002309	0.005216	0.009766
107	0.000311	0.001394	0.003189	0.006259
108	0.000175	0.000813	0.001830	0.003784
109	0.000094	0.000455	0.000974	0.002131
110	0.000049	0.000244	0.000473	0.001100
111	0.000025	0.000125	0.000206	0.000510
112	0.000012	0.000061	0.000078	0.000206
113	0.000005	0.000028	0.000024	0.000068
114	0.000002	0.000012	0.000006	0.000017
115	0.000000	0.000000	0.000000	0.000000

Source: Brown et al. (2001, table 1.1)

B. Proof of Adverse Selection

We first prove that $\hat{a}_1(z) > \hat{a}_2(z)$ for all z, $M \leq z \leq T$. From (9.5), it is seen that $\hat{c}_1(z)$ and $\hat{c}_2(z)$ must intersect at least once over $M < z < T$. Let z_0 be an age at which $\hat{c}_1(z_0) > \hat{c}_2(z_0)$. By (9.4), the sign of $\dot{\hat{c}}(z) > \hat{c}(z)$ at z_0 is equal to the sign of $r_2(z_0) > r_1(z_0)$. Hence, the intersection point is unique, and $\hat{c}_1(z) - \hat{c}_2(z) \gtreqless 0$ as $z \gtreqless z_0$. It follows now from (9.2) that $\hat{a}_1(z) > \hat{a}_2(z)$ for all $M < z < T$.

The pooling rate of return is a weighted average of the two risk-class rates of return, $r_1(z) < r_p(z) < r_2(z)$, provided $\hat{a}_i(z) > 0$, $i = 1, 2$. From (9.2) and (9.5), a sufficient condition for this is that $w(z) + r(z)a(M) - \hat{c}_i(z)$ strictly decreases in z, $i = 1, 2$. By (9.5), this ensures that there exists some z_0, $M < z_0 < T$, such that $w(z) + r(z)a(M) - c_i(z) \gtreqless 0$ as $z \gtreqless z_0$. By (9.2), this implies that $\hat{a}_i(z) > 0$ for all z, $M < z < T$. Assuming that $r_p(z) - r_1(z) > 0$, a sufficient condition for $\hat{a}_1(z) > 0$ is that $w(z) + r(z)a(M)$ is nonincreasing in z. Assuming further that $r_p(z) - r_2(z) < 0$, a more stringent condition is needed to ensure that $\hat{a}_2(z) > 0$ for all $M < z < T$. Thus, the *existence* of a pooling equilibrium depends on parameter configuration.

Since $\hat{c}_1(z) - \hat{c}_2(z) \lesseqgtr 0$ as $z \lesseqgtr z_0$ (where z_0 satisfies $\hat{c}_1(z_0) - \hat{c}_2(z_0) = 0$). Accordingly, optimum retirement age, $\hat{R}_i$, satisfies $\hat{R}_1 \gtreqless \hat{R}_2$ as $\hat{R}_i \gtreqless z_0$, $i = 1, 2$.

CHAPTER 10

Income Uncertainty

10.1 FIRST BEST

It has been assumed throughout that the only uncertainty that the individual faces is longevity risk. It is important to examine the possible effects of other uninsurable uncertainties. Of particular interest is how the interaction of income uncertainty with uncertain longevity affects the purchase of annuities and retirement decisions. Partial insurance against income uncertainty due, for example, to unemployment is commonly provided by public programs. Complementary private insurance, though, is typically unavailable because of adverse selection, moral hazard, and crowding out. Uncertainty that jointly affects survival and income ("disability") is discussed in chapter 16.

Assume that the survival function is known with certainty but that there is uncertainty with respect to future income. Up to age M, wages are $w(z)$, while at age M, prior to retirement, wages have a probability q, $0 < q < 1$, of becoming $w_1(z)$ (high-income state) and probability $1 - q$ of becoming $w_2(z)$ (low-income state), where $w_1(z) > w_2(z)$ for all $M \leq z \leq T$. Consumption is denoted by $c(z)$ for ages before M and by $c_i(z)$ at later ages z, $M \leq z \leq T$, $i = 1, 2$. Let R_i be the age of retirement in state i, $i = 1, 2$. Expected utility is

$$
V = \int_0^M F(z)u(c(z))\,dz + q\left(\int_M^T F(z)u(c_1(z))\,dz - \int_0^{R_1} F(z)e(z)\,dz \right)
$$
$$
+ (1 - q)\left(\int_M^T F(z)u(c_2(z))\,dz - \int_0^{R_2} F(z)e(z)\,dz \right)
$$
$$
= \int_0^M F(z)u(c(z))\,dz + qV_1 + (1 - q)V_2, \tag{10.1}
$$

where V_i,

$$
V_i = \int_M^T F(z)u(c_i(z))\,dz - \int_M^R F(z)e(z)\,dz, \quad i = 1, 2, \tag{10.2}
$$

are the ex post expected utilities in the two states of nature.

The resource constraint is

$$\int_0^M F(z)(w(z) - c(z)) \, dz + q \left(\int_M^R F(z)w_1(z) \, dz - \int_0^T F(z)c_1(z) \, dz \right)$$

$$+ (1-q) \left(\int_M^{R_2} F(z)w_2(z) \, dz - \int_M^T F(z)c_2(z) \, dz \right) = 0. \qquad (10.3)$$

Maximization of (10.1) subject to (10.3) yields the first best: $c(z) = c_1(z) = c_2(z) = c^*$, where

$$c^* = \frac{q \, W_1(R_1^*) + (1-q) \, W_2(R_2^*)}{\bar{z}} \qquad (10.4)$$

and $W_i(R_i^*) = \int_0^M F(z)w(z) \, dz + \int_M^{R_i^*} F(z)w_i(z) \, dz$, $i = 1, 2$.

Optimum retirement ages, R_i^*, are determined by the familiar condition

$$u'(c^*)w_i(R_i^*) - e(R_i^*) = 0, \quad i = 1, 2. \qquad (10.5)$$

Since $w_1(R) > w_2(R)$ for all R, the benefit from a marginal postponement of retirement is higher in state 1 than in state 2, and hence $R_1^* > R_2^*$.

Interestingly, since consumption is equalized across states (entailing an income transfer from the "good" state 1 to state 2), $R_1^* > R_2^*$ implies that while ex ante utility V^*, (10.1), is the same for all individuals, the expost expected utility in state 1, V_1^*, is *lower* than the expected utility in state 2, V_2^* : $V_1^* < V_2^*$.[1] Since utility of consumption and labor disutility are separable, consumption is equalized across states, while retirement is postponed for those in the high-wage state compared to the others, leading to a lower ex-post utility in state 1.

10.2 COMPETITIVE EQUILIBRIUM

It is not surprising that a competitive annuity market cannot attain the first best in this case. Annuities can fully insure against longevity risks (under full information, even when future survival functions are unknown) but cannot implement transfers across states of nature *due to other uninsurable risks*.

In a competitive annuity market consumption before and after age M is independent of age: $c(z) = c$, $0 \leq z \leq M$, and $c_i(z) = c_i$, $M \leq z \leq T$, $i = 1, 2$.

---

[1] In Mirrlees' (1971) optimum income tax model, when utility of consumption and labor disutility are separable, the first best has equal consumption levels, while individuals with higher productivity work more and therefore have lower utilities.

The budget dynamics are given by

$$\dot{a}(z) = r(z)a(z) + w(z) - c, \quad 0 \leq z \leq M, \tag{10.6}$$

$$\dot{a}_i(z) = r(z)a_i(z) + w_i(z) - c_i, \quad M \leq z \leq T, \quad i = 1, 2, \tag{10.7}$$

and $r(z) = f(z)/F(z)$ for all z, $0 \leq z \leq T$. Adding (10.6) and (10.7), we obtain (multiplying by $F(z)$ and integrating by parts over the relevant ranges)

$$\int_0^M F(z)(w(z) - c)\, dz + \int_M^{R_i} F(z)w_i(z)\, dz - c_i \int_M^T F(z)\, dz = 0, \quad i = 1, 2, \tag{10.8}$$

or

$$c_i = \frac{W_i(R_i) - c\int_0^M F(z)\, dz}{\int_M^T F(z)\, dz}, \quad i = 1, 2. \tag{10.9}$$

Clearly, from (10.9), $c_1 > c_2$.

Maximization of (10.2) subject to (10.8) with respect to R_i yields

$$u'(c_i)w_i(R_i) - e(R_i) = 0 \quad i = 1, 2, \tag{10.10}$$

and maximization of expected utility at age 0, V, with respect to c, taking (10.9) into account, yields the condition

$$u'(c) = qu'(c_1) + (1 - q)u'(c_2). \tag{10.11}$$

Optimum consumption prior to age M is a weighted average of optimum consumption in the two states. Equations (9.9)–(9.11) jointly determine the competitive equilibrium: $\hat{c}$, $\hat{c}_i$, and $\hat{R}_i$, $i = 1, 2$. Note that, unlike the first best, $\hat{V}_1 > \hat{V}_2$.

It can further be inferred from (10.6)–(10.8) that the equilibrium level of annuities at age M, $\hat{a}(M) = 1/F(M)\int_0^M F(z)(w(z) - \hat{c})\, dz$ is preserved in later ages, $\hat{a}_i(z) = \hat{a}(M)$ ($\dot{a}_i(z) = 0$), $M \leq z \leq T$, $i = 1, 2$. We reach the same conclusion as with uncertainty about survival functions and full information: *The market for annuities after age M is inactive.* Individuals purchase annuities at early ages, and their consumption adjusts to income realization later in life with no need for further purchase or sale of annuities.

10.3 Moral Hazard

Income uncertainty has various causes, some personal and some reflecting economywide effects. Unemployment, for example, may be voluntary (changing jobs, searching for a job) or imposed. With wage changes, in particular, the individual typically has some influence on the outcome. Thus, the probability q, which was taken as given, may be regarded, to some extent at least, as influenced by individual decisions that involve costs and efforts. The potential conflict that this type of moral hazard raises between social welfare and individual interests is very clear in this context. Since $V_1^* < V_2^*$, an increase in q *decreases* the first-best expected utility. On the other hand, in a competitive equilibrium, $\hat{V}_1 > \hat{V}_2$, and hence an increase in q may be desirable.

CHAPTER 11

Life Insurance and Differentiated Annuities

11.1 BEQUESTS AND ANNUITIES

Regular annuities (sometimes called *life annuities*) provide payouts, fixed or variable, for the duration of the owner's lifetime. No payments are made after the death of the annuitant. There are also *period-certain* annuities, which provide additional payments after death to a beneficiary in the event that the insured individual dies within a specified period after annuitization.[1] Ten-year- and 20-year-certain periods are common (see Brown et al., 2001). Of course, expected benefits during life plus expected payments after death are adjusted to make the price of period-certain annuities commensurate with the price of regular annuities.

These annuities are available in the United Kingdom, where they are called *protected annuities*. It is interesting to quote a description of the motivation for and the stipulations of these annuities from a textbook for actuaries:

> These are usually effected to avoid the disappointment that is often felt in the event of the early death of an annuitant. The calculation of yield closely follows the method used for immediate annuities and this is desirable in order to maintain consistency. The formula would include the appropriate allowance for the additional benefit. (Fisher and Young, 1965, p. 420.)

The behavioral aspect (disappointment) may indeed be a factor in the success of these annuities in the United States and the United Kingdom.

Table 11.1 displays actual quotes of monthly pensions paid against a deposit of $100,000 at different ages. It is taken from Milevsky (2006, p. 111) and represents the best U.S. quotations in 2005.

The terms of period-certain annuities provide a bequest option not offered by regular annuities. It has been argued (e.g., Davidoff, Brown, and Diamond, 2005) that a superior policy for risk-averse individuals who have a bequest motive is to purchase regular annuities (0-year in table 11.1) and a *life insurance* policy. The latter provides a certain amount upon death, while the amount provided by period-certain annuities is random, depending on the age at death.

---

[1] TIAA-CREF, for example, calls these After-Tax Retirement Annuities (ATRA) with death benefits.

TABLE 11.1
Monthly Income from a $100,000 Premium Single-life Pension Annuity (in $).

Period=certain	Age 50		Age 65		Age 70	
	M	F	M	F	M	F
0-year	514	492	655	605	747	677
10-year	509	490	630	592	694	649
20-year	498	484	569	555	591	583

Notes: M, male; F, female. Income starts one month after purchase.

In a competitive market for annuities with full information about longevities, annuity prices vary with annuitants' life expectancies. Such a *separating equilibrium* in the annuity market, together with a competitive market for life insurance, ensures that any combination of period-certain annuities and life insurance is indeed dominated by some combination of regular annuities and life insurance.

The situation is different, however, when individual longevities are *private information* that is not revealed by individuals' choices, and hence each type of annuity is sold at a common price available to all potential buyers. In this kind of *pooling equilibrium*, the price of each type of annuity is equal to the *average* longevity of the buyers of this type of annuity, weighted by the equilibrium amounts purchased. Consequently, these prices are higher than the average expected lifetime of the buyers, reflecting the *adverse selection* caused by the larger amounts of annuities purchased by individuals with higher longevities.[2]

When regular annuities and period-certain annuities are available in the market, self-selection by individuals tends to segment annuity purchasers into different groups. Those with relatively short expected life spans and a high probabilities of early death after annuitization will purchase period-certain annuities (and life insurance). Those with a high life expectancies and a low probabilities of early death will purchase regular annuities (and life insurance). And those with intermediate longevity prospects will hold both types of annuities.

The theoretical implications of our modelling are supported by recent empirical findings reported by Finkelstein and Poterba (2002, 2004), who studied the U.K. annuity market. In a pioneering paper (Finklestein and Poterba, 2004), they test two hypotheses: (1) "Higher-risk individuals self-select into insurance contracts that offer features that, at a given price, are most valuable to them," and (2) "The

---

[2] IT is assumed that the amount of purchased annuities, presumably from different firms, cannot be monitored. This is a standard assumption. See, for example, Brugiavini (1993).

equilibrium pricing of insurance policies reflects variation in the risk pool across different policies." They found that the U.K. data supports both hypotheses.

We provide in this chapter a theoretical underpinning for this observation: *Adverse selection in insurance markets may be revealed by self-selection of different insurance instruments in addition to varying amounts of insurance purchased.*

11.2 FIRST BEST

Consider individuals on the verge of retirement who face uncertain longevities. They derive utility from consumption and from leaving bequests after death. For simplicity, it is assumed that utilities are separable and independent of age. Denote instantaneous utility from consumption by $u(a)$, where a is the flow of consumption and $v(b)$ is the utility from bequests at the level of b. The functions $u(a)$ and $v(b)$ are assumed to be strictly concave and differentiable and satisfy $u'(0) = v'(0) = \infty$ and $u'(\infty) = v'(\infty) = 0$. These assumptions ensure that individuals will choose strictly positive levels of both a and b.

Expected lifetime utility, U, is

$$U = u(a)\bar{z} + v(b), \tag{11.1}$$

where $\bar{z}$ is expected lifetime. Individuals have different longevities represented by a parameter α, $\bar{z} = \bar{z}(\alpha)$. An individual with $\bar{z}(\alpha)$ is termed *type* α. Assume that α varies continuously over the interval $[\underline{\alpha}, \bar{\alpha}]$, $\bar{\alpha} > \underline{\alpha}$. As before, we take a higher α to indicate lower longevity: $\bar{z}'(\alpha) < 0$. Let $G(\alpha)$ be the distribution function of α in the population.

Social welfare, V, is the sum of individuals' expected utilities (or, equivalently, the ex ante expected utility):

$$V = \int_{\underline{\alpha}}^{\bar{\alpha}} [u(a(\alpha))\bar{z}(\alpha) + v(b(\alpha))] \, dG(\alpha), \tag{11.2}$$

where $(a(\alpha), b(\alpha))$ are consumption and bequests, respectively, of type α individuals.

Assume a zero rate of interest, so resources can be carried forward or backward in time at no cost. Hence, given total resources, W, the economy's resource constraint is

$$\int_{\underline{\alpha}}^{\bar{\alpha}} [a(\alpha)\bar{z}(\alpha) + b(\alpha)] \, dG(\alpha) = W. \tag{11.3}$$

Maximization of (11.2) subject to (11.3) yields a unique *first-best* allocation, (a^*, b^*), independent of α, which equalizes the marginal utilities of consumption and bequests:

$$u'(a^*) = v'(b^*). \tag{11.4}$$

Conditions (11.3) and (11.4) jointly determine (a^*, b^*) and the corresponding optimum expected utility of type α individuals, $U^*(\alpha) = u(a^*)\bar{z}(\alpha) + v(b^*)$. Note that while first-best consumption and bequests are equalized across individuals with different longevities, that is, a^* and b^* are independent of α, U^* increases with longevity: $U^{*'}(\alpha) = u(a^*)\bar{z}'(\alpha) < 0$.

11.3 SEPARATING EQUILIBRIUM

Consumption is financed by annuities (for later reference these are called *regular annuities*), while bequests are provided by the purchase of life insurance. Each annuity pays a flow of 1 unit of consumption, contingent on the annuity holder's survival. Denote the price of annuities by p_a. A unit of life insurance pays upon death 1 unit of bequests, and its price is denoted by p_b. Under full information about individual longevities, the price of an annuity in competitive equilibrium varies with the purchaser's longevity, being equal (with a zero interest rate) to life expectancy, $p_a = p_a(\alpha) = \bar{z}(\alpha)$. Since each unit of life insurance pays 1 with certainty, its equilibrium price is unity: $p_b = 1$. This competitive separating equilibrium is always efficient, satisfying condition (11.4), and for a particular income distribution can support the first-best allocation.[3]

11.4 POOLING EQUILIBRIUM

Suppose that longevity is private information. With many suppliers of annuities, only linear price policies (unlike Rothschild-Stiglitz, 1976) are feasible. Hence, in equilibrium, annuities are sold at the same price, p_a, to all individuals.

Assume that all individuals have the same income, W, so their budget constraint is[4]

$$p_a a + p_b b = W. \tag{11.5}$$

---

[3] Individuals who maximize (11.1) subject to budget constraint $\bar{z}(\alpha)a + b = W$ select (a^*, b^*) if and only if $W(\alpha) = \gamma W + (1 - \gamma)b^*$, where $\gamma = \gamma(\alpha) = \dfrac{\bar{z}(\alpha)}{\int_{\underline{\alpha}}^{\bar{\alpha}} \bar{z}(\alpha)\, dG(\alpha)} > 0$. Note that $W(\alpha)$ strictly decreases with α (increases with life expectancy).

[4] As noted above, allowing for different incomes is important for welfare analysis. The joint distribution of incomes and longevity is essential, for example, when considering tax/subsidy policies. Our focus is on the possibility of pooling equilibria with different types of annuities, given *any* income distribution. For simplicity, we assume equal incomes.

Maximization of (11.1) subject to (11.5) yields demand functions for annuities, $\hat{a}(p_a, p_b; \alpha)$, and for life insurance, $\hat{b}(p_a, p_b; \alpha)$.[5] Given our assumptions, $\partial \hat{a}/\partial p_a < 0$, $\partial \hat{a}/\partial \alpha < 0$, $\partial \hat{a}/\partial p_b \gtreqless 0$, $\partial \hat{b}/\partial p_b < 0$, $\partial \hat{b}/\partial \alpha > 0$, $\partial \hat{b}/\partial p_a \gtreqless 0$.

Profits from the sale of annuities, π_a, and from the sale of life insurance, π_b, are

$$\pi_a(p_a, p_b) = \int_{\underline{\alpha}}^{\overline{\alpha}} (p_a - \bar{z}(\alpha))\hat{a}(p_a, p_b; \alpha)\, dG(\alpha) \tag{11.6}$$

and

$$\pi_b(p_a, p_b) = \int_{\underline{\alpha}}^{\overline{\alpha}} (p_b - 1)\hat{b}(p_a, p_b; \alpha)\, dG(\alpha). \tag{11.7}$$

A pooling equilibrium is a pair of prices $(\hat{p}_a, \hat{p}_b)$ that satisfy $\pi_a(\hat{p}_a, \hat{p}_b) = \pi_b(\hat{p}_a, \hat{p}_b) = 0$.

Clearly, $\hat{p}_b = 1$ because marginal costs of a life insurance policy are constant and equal to 1. In view of (11.6),

$$\hat{p}_a = \frac{\int_{\underline{\alpha}}^{\overline{\alpha}} \bar{z}(\alpha)\hat{a}(\hat{p}_a, 1; \alpha)\, dG(\alpha)}{\int_{\underline{\alpha}}^{\overline{\alpha}} \hat{a}(\hat{p}_a, 1; \alpha)\, dG(\alpha)}. \tag{11.8}$$

The equilibrium price of annuities is an average of marginal costs (equal to life expectancy), weighted by the equilibrium amounts of annuities.

It is seen from (11.8) that $\bar{z}(\bar{\alpha}) < \hat{p}_a < \bar{z}(\underline{\alpha})$. Furthermore, since $\hat{a}$ and $\bar{z}(\alpha)$ decrease with α, $\hat{p}_a > E(\bar{z}) = \int_{\underline{\alpha}}^{\overline{\alpha}} \bar{z}(\alpha)\, dG(\alpha)$. The equilibrium price of annuities is higher than the population's average expected lifetime, reflecting the adverse selection present in a pooling equilibrium.

Regarding price dynamics out of equilibrium, we follow the standard assumption that the sign of the price of each good changes in the opposite direction to the sign of profits from sales of this good.

The following assumption about the relation between the elasticity of demand for annuities and longevity ensures the uniqueness and stability of the pooling equilibrium. Let

$$\varepsilon_{ap_a}(p_a, p_b; \alpha) = \frac{p_a}{\hat{a}(p_a, p_b; \alpha)} \frac{\partial \hat{a}(p_a, p_b; \alpha)}{\partial p_a}$$

be the price elasticity of the demand for annuities (at a given α). Assume that for any (p_a, p_b), ε_{ap_a} is nondecreasing in α. Under this assumption, the pooling equilibrium, $\hat{p}_a$, satisfying (11.8) and $\hat{p}_b = 1$ is unique and stable.

---

[5] The dependence on W is suppressed.

To see this, observe that the solution $\hat{p}_a$ and $\hat{p}_b = 1$ satisfying (11.6) and (11.7) is unique and stable if the matrix

$$\begin{bmatrix} \partial\pi_a/\partial a & \partial\pi_a/\partial p_b \\ \partial\pi_b/\partial p_a & \partial\pi_b/\partial p_b \end{bmatrix} \tag{11.9}$$

is strictly *positive-definite* at $(\hat{p}_a, 1)$. It can be shown that $\partial\pi_b/\partial p_a = 0$, $\partial\pi_b/\partial p_b = \hat{b}(\hat{p}_a, 1) > 0$,

$$\frac{\partial\pi_a}{\partial p_a} = \hat{a}(\hat{p}_a, 1) + \int_{\underline{\alpha}}^{\bar{\alpha}} (\hat{p}_a - \bar{z}(\alpha)) \frac{\partial\hat{a}(\hat{p}_a, 1; \alpha)}{\partial p_a} \, dG(\alpha),$$

and

$$\partial\pi_a/\partial p_b = \int_{\underline{\alpha}}^{\bar{\alpha}} (\hat{p}_a - \bar{z}(\alpha)) \frac{\partial\hat{a}(\hat{p}_a, 1; \alpha)}{\partial p_b} \, dG(\alpha),$$

where $\hat{a}(p_a, 1) = \int_{\underline{\alpha}}^{\bar{\alpha}} \hat{a}(p_a, 1; \alpha) \, dG(\alpha)$ and $\hat{b}(p_a, 1) = \int_{\underline{\alpha}}^{\bar{\alpha}} \hat{b}(p_a, 1; \alpha) \, dG(\alpha)$ are aggregate demands for annuities and life insurance, respectively.

Rewrite

$$\int_{\underline{\alpha}}^{\bar{\alpha}} (\hat{p}_a - \bar{z}(\alpha)) \frac{\partial\hat{a}(\hat{p}_a, 1; \alpha)}{\partial p_a} \, dG(\alpha)$$

$$= \frac{1}{\hat{p}_a} \int_{\underline{\alpha}}^{\bar{\alpha}} (\hat{p}_a - \bar{z}(\alpha)) \, \hat{a}(\hat{p}_a, 1; \alpha)\varepsilon_{p_a a}(\hat{p}_a, 1; \alpha) \, dG(\alpha). \tag{11.10}$$

By (11.6), $\hat{p}_a - \bar{z}(\alpha)$ changes sign once over $(\underline{\alpha}, \bar{\alpha})$, say at $\tilde{\alpha}$, $\underline{\alpha} < \tilde{\alpha} < \bar{\alpha}$, such that $\hat{p}_a - \bar{z}(\alpha) \lesseqgtr 0$ as $\alpha \lesseqgtr \tilde{\alpha}$. It now follows from the above assumption about the monotonicity of $\varepsilon_{p_a a}$ and from (11.6) that

$$\int_{\underline{\alpha}}^{\bar{\alpha}} (\hat{p}_a - \bar{z}(\alpha)) \frac{\partial\hat{a}(\hat{p}_a, 1; \alpha)}{\partial p_a} \, dG(\alpha)$$

$$\geq \frac{\varepsilon_{p_a a}(\hat{p}_a, 1; \tilde{\alpha})}{\hat{p}_a} \int_{\underline{\alpha}}^{\bar{\alpha}} (\hat{p}_a - \bar{z}(\alpha))\hat{a}(\hat{p}_a, 1; \alpha) \, dG(\alpha) = 0. \tag{11.11}$$

It follows that $\partial\pi_a(\hat{p}_a, 1)/\partial p_a > 0$, which implies that (11.9) is positive-definite.

Figure 11.1 (drawn for $\partial\pi_a/\partial p_b < 0$) displays this result.

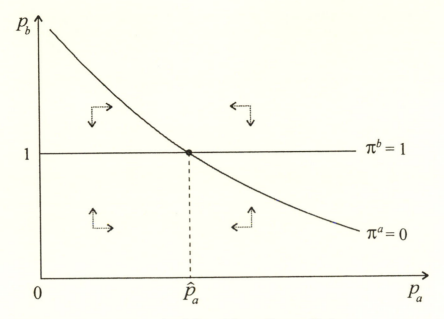

Figure 11.1. Uniqueness and stability of the pooling equilibrium.

11.5 Period-certain Annuities and Life Insurance

We have assumed that annuities provide payouts for the duration of the owner's lifetime and that no payments are made after the death of the annuitant. We called these regular annuities. There are also period-certain annuities that provide additional payments to a designated beneficiary after the death of the insured individual, provided death occurs within a specified period after annuitization. Ten-year- and 20-year-certain periods are common, and more annuitants choose them than regular annuities (see Brown et al., 2001). Of course, benefits during life plus expected payments after death are adjusted to make the price of period-certain annuities commensurate with the price of regular annuities.

(a) The Inferiority of Period-certain Annuities Under Full Information

Suppose that there are regular annuities and X-year-certain annuities (in short, X-annuities) that offer a unit flow of consumption while an individual is alive and an additional amount if they die before age X. We continue to denote the amount of regular annuities by a and the amount of X-annuities by a_x. The additional payment that an X-annuity offers if death occurs before age X is δ, $\delta > 0$.

Consider the first-best allocation when both types of annuities are available. Social welfare, V, is

$$V = \int_{\underline{\alpha}}^{\bar{\alpha}} [u(a(\alpha)+a_x(\alpha))\bar{z}(\alpha)+v(b(\alpha)+\delta a_x(\alpha))p(\alpha)+v(b(\alpha))(1-p(\alpha))]\,dG(\alpha),$$

(11.12)

and the resource constraint is

$$\int_{\underline{\alpha}}^{\bar{\alpha}} [(a(\alpha) + a_x(\alpha))\bar{z}(\alpha) + \delta a_x p(\alpha) + b(\alpha)]\,dG(\alpha) = W,$$

(11.13)

where $p(\alpha)$ is the probability that a type α individual (with longevity $\bar{z}(\alpha)$) will die before age X.[6] Maximization of (11.12) subject to (11.13) yields $a_x(\alpha) = 0, \underline{\alpha} < \alpha < \bar{\alpha}$. Thus, the first best has no X-annuities. This outcome also characterizes any competitive equilibrium under full information about individual longevities. *In a competitive separating equilibrium, the random bequest option offered by X-annuities is dominated by regular annuities and life insurance which jointly provide for nonrandom consumption and bequests.*

However, we shall now show that X-annuities may be held by individuals in a pooling equilibrium. Self-selection leads to a market equilibrium segmented by the two types of annuities: Individuals with low longevities and a high probability of early death purchase only X-annuities and life insurance, while individuals with high longevities and low probabilities of early death purchase only regular annuities and life insurance. In a range of intermediate longevities individuals hold both types of annuities.

(b) Pooling Equilibrium with Period-certain Annuities

Suppose first that only X-annuities and life insurance are available. Denote the price of X-annuities by p_a^x. The individual's budget

---

[6] Let $f(z, \alpha)$ be the probability of death at age z: $f(z, \alpha) = (\partial/\partial z)(1 - F(z, \alpha)) = -(\partial F/\partial z)(z, \alpha)$. Then $p(\alpha) = \int_0^X f(z, \alpha)\,dz$. The typical stipulations of X-annuities are that the holder of an X-annuity who dies at age z, $0 < z < x$, receives payment proportional to the *remaining period* until age X, $X - z$. Thus, expected payment is proportional to $\int_0^X (X - z) f(z, \alpha)\,dz$. In our formulation, therefore, δ should be interpreted as the *certainty equivalence* of this amount.

constraint is

$$p_a^x a_x + b_x = W, \tag{11.14}$$

where b_x is the amount of life insurance purchased jointly with X-annuities. The equilibrium price of life insurance is, as before, unity.

For any α, expected utility, U_x, is given by

$$U_x = u(a_x)\bar{z}(\alpha) + v(b_x + \delta a_x)p(\alpha) + v(b_x)(1 - p(\alpha)). \tag{11.15}$$

Maximization of (11.15) subject to (11.14) yields (strictly) positive amounts $\hat{a}_x(p_a^x; \alpha)$ and $\hat{b}_x(p_a^x; \alpha)$.[7] It can be shown that $\partial\hat{a}_x/\partial p_a^x < 0$, $\partial\hat{a}_x/\partial\alpha < 0$, $\partial\hat{b}_x/\partial\alpha > 0$ and $\partial\hat{b}_x/\partial p_a^x \gtreqless 0$. Optimum expected utility, $\hat{U}_x$, may increase or decrease with α: $(d\hat{U}_x/d\alpha) = u(\hat{a}_x)\,\bar{z}'(\alpha) + [v(\hat{b}_x + \delta\hat{a}_x) - v(\hat{b}_x)]\,p'(\alpha)$. We shall assume that $p'(\alpha) > 0$, which is reasonable (though not necessary) since $\bar{z}'(\alpha) < 0$.[8] Hence, the sign of $d\hat{U}_x/d\alpha$ is indeterminate.

Total revenue from annuity sales is $p_a^x\hat{a}_x(p_a^x)$, where $\hat{a}_x(p_a^x) = \int_{\underline{\alpha}}^{\overline{\alpha}}\hat{a}_x(p_a^x; \alpha)\,dG(\alpha)$ is the aggregate demand for X-annuities. Expected payout is $\int_{\underline{\alpha}}^{\overline{\alpha}}(\bar{z}(\alpha) + \delta p(\alpha))\hat{a}_x(p_a^x; \alpha)\,dG(\alpha)$. The condition for zero expected profits is therefore

$$\hat{p}_a^x = \frac{\int_{\underline{\alpha}}^{\overline{\alpha}}(\bar{z}(\alpha) + \delta p(\alpha))\hat{a}_x(\hat{p}_a^x; \alpha)\,dG(\alpha)}{\int_{\underline{\alpha}}^{\overline{\alpha}}\hat{a}_x(\hat{p}_a^x; \alpha)}, \tag{11.16}$$

where $\hat{p}_a^x$ is the equilibrium price of X-annuities. It is seen to be an average of longevities plus δ times the probability of early death, weighted by the equilibrium amounts of X-annuities. As with regular annuities, assume that the demand elasticity of X-annuities increases with α. In addition to this assumption, a sufficient condition for the uniqueness and stability of a pooling equilibrium with X-annuities is that $\hat{p}_a^x - \bar{z}(\alpha) - \delta p(\alpha)$ increases with α. This is not a vacuous assumption because $\bar{z}'(\alpha) < 0$ and $p'(\alpha) > 0$. It states that the first effect dominates the second. Following the same argument as above,[9] it can be shown that the pooling equilibrium, $\hat{p}_a^x$, satisfying (11.16) and $\hat{p}_b = 1$, is unique and stable.

---

[7] Henceforth, we suppress the price of life insurance, $\hat{p}_b = 1$, and the dependence on δ.

[8] For example, with $F(z, \alpha) = e^{-\alpha z}$, $f(z, \alpha) = \alpha e^{-\alpha z}$ and $p(\alpha) = \int_0^x f(z, \alpha)\,dz = 1 - e^{-\alpha x}$, which implies $p'(\alpha) > 0$.

[9] The specific condition is $\hat{a}_x(\hat{p}_a^x) + \int_{\underline{\alpha}}^{\overline{\alpha}}(\hat{p}_a^x - \bar{z}(\alpha) - \delta p(\alpha))\,(\partial\hat{a}_x/\partial p_a^x)(p_a^x; \alpha)\,dG(\alpha) > 0$. Positive monotonicity of the price elasticity of $\hat{a}_x$ with respect to α is a sufficient condition.

11.6 Mixed Pooling Equilibrium

Now suppose that the market offers regular and X-annuities as well as life insurance. We shall show that, depending on the distribution $G(\alpha)$, *self-selection* of individuals in the pooling equilibrium may lead to the following market segmentation: Those with high longevities and low probabilities of early death purchase only regular annuities, those with low longevities and high probabilities of early death purchase only X-annuities, and individuals with intermediate longevities and probabilities of early death hold both types. We call this a *mixed pooling equilibrium*.

Given p_a, p_a^x, $\bar{z}(\alpha)$, and $p(\alpha)$, the individual maximizes expected utility,

$$U = u(a + a_x)\bar{z}(\alpha) + v(b + \delta a_x)p(\alpha) + v(b)(1 - p(\alpha)), \qquad (11.17)$$

subject to the budget constraint

$$p_a a + p_a^x a_x + b = W. \qquad (11.18)$$

The first-order conditions for an interior maximum are

$$u'(\hat{a} + \hat{a}_x)\bar{z}(\alpha) - \lambda p_a = 0, \qquad (11.19)$$

$$u'(\hat{a} + \hat{a}_x)\bar{z}(\alpha) + v'(\hat{b} + \delta \hat{a}_x)\delta p(\alpha) - \lambda p_a^x = 0, \qquad (11.20)$$

$$v'(\hat{b} + \delta \hat{a}_x)p(\alpha) + v'(\hat{b})(1 - p(\alpha)) - \lambda = 0, \qquad (11.21)$$

where $\lambda > 0$ is the Lagrangean associated with (11.18). Equations (11.18)–(11.21) jointly determine positive amounts $\hat{a}(p_a, p_a^x; \alpha)$, $\hat{a}_x(p_a, p_a^x; \alpha)$, and $\hat{b}(p_a, p_a^x; \alpha)$.

Note first that from (11.19)–(11.21), it follows that

$$p_a < p_a^x < p_a + \delta \qquad (11.22)$$

is a necessary condition for an interior solution. When the left-hand-side inequality in (11.22) does not hold, then X-annuities, each paying a flow of 1 while alive *plus* δ with probability p after death, dominate regular annuities for all α. When the right-hand-side inequality in (11.22) does not hold, then regular annuities and life insurance dominate X-annuities because the latter pay a flow of 1 while alive and δ after death with probability $p < 1$.

Second, given our assumption that $u'(0) = v'(0) = \infty$, it follows that $\hat{b} > 0$ and *either* $\hat{a} > 0$ or $\hat{a}_x > 0$ for all α. It is impossible to have $\hat{a} = \hat{a}_x = 0$ at any α.

$\hat{a} > 0, \hat{a}_x = 0$

Condition (11.20) becomes an inequality

$$u'(\hat{a})\bar{z} + v'(\hat{b})\delta p(\alpha) - \lambda p_a^x \leq 0, \tag{11.23}$$

while (11.19) and (11.21) (with $\hat{a}_x = 0$) continue to hold. From these conditions it follows that in this case,

$$p(\alpha) \leq \frac{p_a^x - p_a}{\delta}. \tag{11.24}$$

Denote the right hand side of (11.24) by $p(\alpha_0)$. Since $p(\alpha)$ increases in α, it follows that individuals with $\underline{\alpha} \leq \alpha \leq \alpha_0$ purchase only regular annuities (and life insurance).

$\hat{a} = 0, \; \hat{a}_x > 0$

Condition (11.19) becomes an inequality,

$$u'(\hat{a}_x)\bar{z}(\alpha) - \lambda p_a \leq 0, \tag{11.25}$$

while (11.20) and (11.21) continue to hold (with $\hat{a} = 0$).
Let

$$\varphi(\alpha) = \frac{1}{1 + \dfrac{v'(\hat{b} + \delta\hat{a}_x)}{v'(\hat{b})}\left(\dfrac{1 - p(\alpha_0)}{p(\alpha_0)}\right)}. \tag{11.26}$$

It is seen that at $\alpha = \alpha_0$, $\varphi(\alpha_0) = p(\alpha_0)$. From (11.19)–(11.21) it can be further deduced that $p(\alpha) = \varphi(\alpha)$ at any interior solution ($\hat{a} > 0$, $\hat{a}_x > 0$). As α increases from α_0, $\hat{a}(\alpha)$ decreases, while $\hat{a}_x(\alpha)$ increases (see appendix). Let $\hat{a}(\alpha_1) = 0$ for some α_1, $\alpha_0 < \alpha_1 < \bar{\alpha}$. From (11.25), (11.20), and (11.21), it can be seen that $p(\alpha) \geq \varphi(\alpha)$ whenever $\hat{a} = 0$ ($\hat{a}_x > 0$). It follows that if $\varphi(\alpha)$ is nonincreasing with α for all $\alpha > \alpha_1$, then all individuals with $\alpha_1 < \alpha < \bar{\alpha}$ hold only X-annuities (and life insurance). A sufficient condition for this to hold is that $v''(x)/v'(x)$ is nondecreasing with x (note that exponential and power functions satisfy this assumption). Under these assumptions, all individuals with $\alpha_1 < \alpha < \bar{\alpha}$ hold only X-annuities.

The proof is straightforward: $\varphi(\alpha)$ is nonincreasing in α if and only if $v'(\hat{b} + \delta\hat{a}_x)/v'(\hat{b})$ is nondecreasing in α. Using the budget constraint

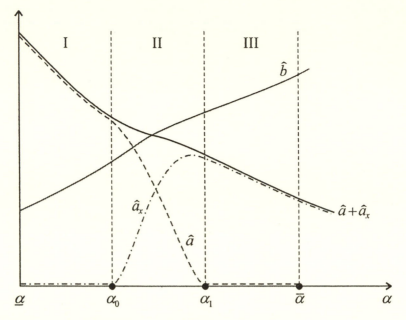

Figure 11.2. Optimum annuity holdings.

(11.18) with $\hat{a} = 0$,

$$\frac{\partial}{\partial \alpha}\left(\frac{v'(\hat{b} + \delta\hat{a}_x)}{v'(\hat{b})}\right) = \frac{v'(\hat{b} + \delta\hat{a}_x)}{v'(\hat{b})}\left[\left(\frac{v''(\hat{b})}{v'(\hat{b})} - \frac{v''(\hat{b} + \delta\hat{a}_x)}{v'(\hat{b} + \delta\hat{a}_x)}\right) p_a^x\right.$$

$$\left. + \delta\frac{v''(\hat{b} + \delta\hat{a}_x)}{v'(\hat{b} + \delta\hat{a}_x)}\right] \frac{\partial\hat{a}_x}{\partial \alpha} \tag{11.27}$$

Since $\partial\hat{a}_x/\partial\alpha < 0$ (see appendix), the above assumption is seen to ensure that (11.27) is strictly positive, implying that $\varphi(\alpha)$ decreases with α.

The pattern of optimum annuity holdings and life insurance is shown schematically in figure 11.2. For justification of this pattern in the three regions I–III, see the appendix to this chapter.

Equilibrium prices satisfy a zero expected profits condition for each type of annuity, taking into account the self-selection discussed above: $\pi_a(\hat{p}_a, \hat{p}_a^x, 1) = \pi_a^x(\hat{p}_a, \hat{p}_a^x, 1) = \pi_b(\hat{p}_a, \hat{p}_a^x, 1) = 0$. These conditions can be written (suppressing $\hat{p}_b = 1$)

$$\hat{p}_a = \frac{\int_{\underline{\alpha}}^{\overline{\alpha}} \bar{z}(\alpha)\hat{a}(\hat{p}_a, \hat{p}_a^x; \alpha)\, dG(\alpha)}{\int_{\underline{\alpha}}^{\overline{\alpha}} \hat{a}(\hat{p}_a, \hat{p}_a^x; \alpha)\, dG(\alpha)} \tag{11.28}$$

and

$$\hat{p}_a^x = \frac{\int_{\underline{\alpha}}^{\overline{\alpha}}(\bar{z}(\alpha) + \delta p(\alpha))\hat{a}(\hat{p}_a, \hat{p}_a^x; \alpha)\, dG(\alpha)}{\int_{\underline{\alpha}}^{\overline{\alpha}}\hat{a}(\hat{p}_a, \hat{p}_a^x; \alpha)\, dG(\alpha)} \tag{11.29}$$

In section 11.4 we stated conditions that ensure uniqueness and stability of the pooling equilibrium. Similar conditions can be formulated to ensure that a mixed pooling equilibrium has the same properties.[10]

11.7 SUMMARY

Recapitulation: In efficient, full-information equilibria, the holdings of any period-certain annuities and life insurance are dominated by holdings of some combination of regular annuities and life insurance. However, when information about longevities is private, a competitive pooling equilibrium may support the coexistence of differentiated annuities and life insurance, with some individuals holding only one type of annuity and some holding both types of annuities.

Reassuringly, Finkelstein and Poterba (2004) find evidence of such self-selection in the U.K. annuity market. More specifically, our analysis suggests a hypothesis complementary to their observation of self-selection: Those with high longevities hold regular annuities, those with low longevities hold period-certain annuities, and there are mixed holdings for intermediate longevities.

---

[10] These conditions ensure that the matrix of the partial derivatives of expected profits with respect to p_a, p_a^x, and p_b is positive-definite around $\hat{p}_a$, $\hat{p}_a^x$ and $\hat{p}_b = 1$.

Appendix

We derive here the dependence of the demands for annuities and life insurance on α. Maximizing (11.17) subject to the budget constraint (11.18) yields solutions $\hat{a}$, $\hat{a}_x$, and $\hat{b}$ Given our assumption that $v'(0) = \infty$, $\hat{b} > 0$ for all α. Regarding annuities, we distinguish three cases: (I) $\hat{a} \geq 0$, $\hat{a}_x = 0$; (II) $\hat{a} \geq 0$, $\hat{a}_x \geq 0$, and (III) $\hat{a} = 0$, $\hat{a}_x \geq 0$.

(I) $\hat{a} \geq 0$, $\hat{a}_x = 0$ $(\underline{\alpha} < \alpha < \alpha_0)$

$$u'(\hat{a})\bar{z}(\alpha) - v'(\hat{b})p_a = 0, \tag{11A.1}$$

$$W - p_a\hat{a} - \hat{b} = 0. \tag{11A.2}$$

Differentiating totally,

$$\frac{\partial\hat{a}}{\partial\alpha} = -\frac{u'(\hat{a})\bar{z}'(\alpha)}{\Delta_1} < 0, \quad \frac{\partial\hat{b}}{\partial\alpha} = \frac{p_a u'(\hat{a})\bar{z}'(\alpha)}{\Delta_1} > 0, \tag{11A.3}$$

$$\left(\frac{\partial\hat{a}}{\partial p_a} \gtrless 0\right),$$

where

$$\Delta_1 = u''(\hat{a})\bar{z}(\alpha) + v''(\hat{b})p_a^2 < 0. \tag{11A.4}$$

(II) $\hat{a} \geq 0$, $\hat{a}_x \geq 0$ $(\alpha_0 < \alpha < \alpha_1)$

Equations (11.19)–(11.21) and the budget constraint hold:

$$u'(\hat{a} + \hat{a}_x)\bar{z}(\alpha) - \lambda p_a = 0, \tag{11A.5}$$

$$u'(\hat{a} + \hat{a}_x)\bar{z}(\alpha) + v'(\hat{b} + \delta\hat{a}_x)\delta p(\alpha) - \lambda p_a^x = 0, \tag{11A.6}$$

$$v'(\hat{b} + \delta\hat{a}_x)p(\alpha) + v'(\hat{b})(1 - p(\alpha)) - \lambda = 0, \tag{11A.7}$$

$$W - p_a\hat{a} - p_a^x\hat{a}_x - \hat{b} = 0 \tag{11A.8}$$

(11A.5)–(11A.8) are four equations in $\hat{a}$, $\hat{a}_x$, $\hat{b}$, and λ. The second-order conditions can be shown to hold:

$$\Delta_2 = -\left(u''(\hat{a} + \hat{a}_x)\bar{z}(\alpha)\right)^2 - u''(\hat{a} + \hat{a}_x)\bar{z}(\alpha)[v''(\hat{b} + \delta\hat{a}_x)p(\alpha)(p_a^x - p_a - \delta)^2$$

$$+ v''(\hat{b} + \delta\hat{a}_x)p(\alpha)p_a(p_a^x - \delta) + v''(\hat{b})(1 - p(\alpha))(p_a^x - p_a)^2$$

$$+ v''(\hat{b})(1 - p(\alpha))p_a p_a^x] - p_a^2 v''(\hat{b} + \delta\hat{a}_x)\delta^2 p(\alpha)v''(\hat{b})(1 - p(\alpha)) < 0,$$

$$\text{(11A.9)}$$

provided $p_a^x - \delta > 0$.

The signs of $\partial\hat{a}/\partial\alpha$ and $\partial\hat{a}_x/\partial\alpha$ cannot be established for all α in this range without further restrictions. However, at $\alpha = \alpha_0$, differentiating (11A.5)–(11A.8) totally with respect to α, using (11.24), $p(\alpha_0) = p_a^x - p_a/\delta$, we obtain after some manipulations:

$$\frac{\partial\hat{a}}{\partial\alpha} = \frac{-1}{\Delta_2}[v''(\hat{b})(p_a^x - p_a)(p_a^x - p_a - \delta)u'(\hat{a})\bar{z}'(\alpha_0)$$

$$\text{(11A.10)}$$

$$+ (u''(\hat{a})\bar{z}'(\alpha) + v''(\hat{b})p_a^2)\, v'(\hat{b})\delta p'(\alpha_0)] < 0,$$

$$\frac{\partial\hat{a}_x}{\partial\alpha} = \frac{-1}{\Delta_2}[u''(\hat{a})\bar{z}(\alpha) + p_a^2 v''(\hat{b})]v'(\hat{b})\delta p'(\alpha_0) > 0, \quad \text{(11A.11)}$$

and $\partial\hat{b}/\partial\alpha > 0$, where

$$\Delta_2 = (p_a^x - p_a)(p_a^x - p_a - \delta)(u''(\hat{a})\bar{z}'(\alpha) + p_a^2 v''(\hat{b}))v''(\hat{b}) < 0. \quad \text{(11A.12)}$$

Furthermore,

$$\frac{\partial\hat{a}}{\partial\alpha} + \frac{\partial\hat{a}_x}{\partial\alpha} = \frac{-1}{\Delta_2}(p_a^x - p_a)(p_a^x - p_a - \delta)v''(\hat{b})u'(\hat{a})\bar{z}'(\alpha_0) < 0. \quad \text{(11A.13)}$$

As α increases from $\alpha = \alpha_0$, $\hat{a}$ decreases, $\hat{a}_x$ increases, and $\hat{a} + \hat{a}_x$ decreases, while $\hat{b}$ increases.

This justifies the general pattern displayed in figure 11.2 at α_0. Individuals with $\alpha > \alpha_0$ hold positive amounts of *both* types of annuities and, while substituting regular for period-certain annuities, decrease the total amount of annuities as longevity decreases.

We cannot establish that the direction of these changes is monotone at all α, but we have proved the main point: Generally, X-annuities may be held in a pooling equilibrium.

(III) $\hat{a} = 0$, $\hat{a}_x \geq 0$ $(\alpha_1 < \alpha < \bar{\alpha})$

$$u'(\hat{a}_x)\bar{z}(\alpha) + v'(\hat{b} + \delta\hat{a}_x)\delta p(\alpha) - \lambda p_a^x = 0, \tag{11A.14}$$

$$v'(\hat{b} + \delta\hat{a}_x)p(\alpha) + v'(\hat{b})(1 - p(\alpha)) - \lambda = 0, \tag{11A.15}$$

$$W - p_a^x\hat{a}_x - \hat{b} = 0. \tag{11A.16}$$

The second-order condition is satisfied:

$$\Delta_3 = -u''(\hat{a}_x)\bar{z}(\alpha) - v''(\hat{b}+\delta\hat{a}_x)(p_a^x-\delta)^2 p(\alpha) - p_a^{x^2} v''(\hat{b}+\delta\hat{a}_x)(1-p(\alpha)) > 0 \tag{11A.17}$$

and

$$\frac{\partial \hat{a}_x}{\partial \alpha} = \frac{1}{\Delta_3}[u'(\hat{a}_x)\bar{z}'(\alpha) + (p_a^x v'(\hat{b}+\delta\hat{a}_x) - v'(\hat{b}+\delta\hat{a})(p_a^x-\delta))p'(\alpha)], \tag{11A.18}$$

$$\frac{\partial \hat{b}}{\partial \alpha} = \frac{p_a^x}{\Delta_3}[-u'(\hat{a}_x)\bar{z}'(\alpha) + (p_a^x - \delta)v'(\hat{b}+\delta\hat{a}_x) + p_a^x v'(\hat{b}+\delta\hat{a}_x)]. \tag{11A.19}$$

It is seen from (11A.18) and (11A.19) that $\partial\hat{a}_x/\partial\alpha < 0$ and $\partial\hat{b}/\partial\alpha > 0$, provided $p_a^x - \delta > 0$.

CHAPTER 12

Annuities, Longevity, and Aggregate Savings

12.1 Changes in Longevity and Aggregate Savings

In chapter 5 it was shown that when an increase in survival probabilities is tilted toward older ages, then individuals save more during their working years in order to support a longer retirement. Chosen retirement ages also rise with longevity, but this was shown to compensate only partially for the need to decrease consumption. In this chapter we shift the emphasis from individual savings to aggregate savings.

When aggregating the response of individuals to changes in longevity, one has to take into account that over time these changes affect the population's age density function (this is called the *age composition effect* in contrast to the response of individuals, called the *behavioral effect*). The direction of the change in this function reflects two opposite effects. First, an increase in survival rates increases the size of all age cohorts, particularly in older ages. Second, for given age-specific birthrates, an increase in survival probabilities raises the population's long-run growth rate which, in turn, increases the relative weight of younger cohorts in the population's age density function. Since older ages are typically retirees who are dissavers, while younger ages are savers, the first effect tends to reduce aggregate savings while the second effect tends to raise their level. We shall provide conditions that ensure that the latter effect is dominant.

The dynamics of demographic processes generated by a change in survival probabilities is quite complex. There exists, however, a well-developed theory on the dependence of *steady-state age density distributions* on the underlying parameters (e.g., Coale, 1972). The analysis below builds on this theory.

The relation between life expectancy and aggregate savings has been explored empirically in many studies (e.g., Kinugasa and Mason, 2007; Miles, 1999; Deaton and Paxson, 2000; and Lee, Mason, and Miller, 2001). All these articles find a positive correlation between life expectancy and aggregate savings. Since these studies have no explicit aggregation of individuals' response functions, they do not attempt to identify separately the direction and size of the behavioral effect and the age composition effect. Furthermore, it is shown below that a change in life expectancy is, in itself, inadequate to predict individuals' response and hence aggregate changes. This response depends on more specific assumptions about the age-related changes in survival probabilities.

The existence of a competitive annuity market is crucial for individual decisions on savings and retirement. In the absence of this market, these decisions have to take into account the existence of *unintended bequests*, that is, assets left at death because individuals do not want to outlive their resources. Under these circumstances, an uncertain lifetime generates a random distribution of bequests that become initial endowments of a subsequent generation. Thus, analysis of the long-term effects of changes in longevity has to focus on the (ergodic) evolution of the distribution of these bequests and endowments. Section 12.6 provides an example of such an analysis.

12.2 Longevity and Individual Savings

In chapter 4 it was shown that individuals' optimum consumption, c^*, is given by

$$c^* = -\frac{\int_0^{R^*} w(z) F(z, \alpha) \, dz}{\bar{z}} \tag{12.1}$$

and optimum retirement age, R^*, is determined by the condition

$$u'(c^*) w(R^*) - e(R^*) = 0, \tag{12.2}$$

where $\bar{z}(\alpha) = \int_0^\infty F(z, \alpha) \, dz$ is expected lifetime. A decrease in α is taken to increase survival probabilities, $\partial F(z, \alpha)/\partial \alpha < 0$, for all z.

Recall that $\mu(z, \alpha)$ is the proportional change in the survival function at age z due to a small change in α:

$$\mu(z, \alpha) = \frac{1}{F(z, \alpha)} \frac{\partial F(z, \alpha)}{\partial \alpha} \quad (< 0).$$

Differentiating (12.1) and (12.2) totally with respect to α, it was shown that *when* $\mu(z, \alpha)$ *decreases with* z (equivalently, that a decrease in α decreases the hazard rate), *then* $dc^*/d\alpha > 0$ *and* $dR^*/d\alpha < 0$.

12.3 Longevity and Aggregate Savings

Suppose that the population grows at a constant rate, g. The *steady-state* age density function of the population, denoted $h(z, \alpha, g)$, is given by[1]

$$h(z, \alpha, g) = me^{-gz}F(z, \alpha), \tag{12.3}$$

where $m = 1/\int_0^\infty e^{-gz}F(z, \alpha)\,dz$ is the birthrate.

The growth rate g, in turn, is determined by the second fundamental equation of stable population theory:

$$\int_0^\infty e^{-gz}F(z, \alpha)b(z)\,dz = 1, \tag{12.4}$$

where $b(z)$ is the age-specific birthrate (fertility) function.

The magnitude of g depends implicitly on the form of the survival and fertility functions, $F(z, \alpha)$ and $b(z)$, respectively. It can be determined explicitly in some special cases. For example, with $F(z, \alpha) = e^{-\alpha z}$ and $b(z) = b > 0$, constant, for all $z \geq 0$, (12.4) yields $g = b - \alpha$. The population growth rate is equal to the difference between the birthrate and the mortality rate.

The effect on g of a change in α can be determined by totally differentiating (12.4):

$$\frac{dg}{d\alpha} = \frac{\int_0^\infty e^{-gz}\dfrac{\partial F(z, \alpha)}{\partial \alpha}b(z)\,dz}{\int_0^\infty e^{-gz}zF(z, \alpha)b(z)\,dz} < 0. \tag{12.5}$$

An increase in longevity is seen to raise the steady-state growth rate of the population. In the exponential example, substituting $(1/F)(\partial F/\partial \alpha) = -z$ into (12.5), we obtain $dg/d\alpha = -1$.

Individual savings at age z, $s^*(z)$, are

$$s^*(z) = \begin{cases} w(z) - c^*, & 0 \leq z \leq R^*, \\ -c^*, & R^* \leq z \leq \infty. \end{cases} \tag{12.6}$$

[1] Equations (12.3) and (12.4) are derived as follows (see Coale, 1972): Let the current number of age-z females be $n(z)$, while the total number is N. When the population grows at a rate g, the number of females z periods ago was Ne^{-gz}. If m is the birthrate, then z periods ago mNe^{-gz} females were born. Given the survival function $F(z, \alpha)$,

$$h(z, \alpha, g) = \frac{n(z)}{N} = \frac{Ne^{-gz}mF(z, \alpha)}{N} = me^{-gz}F(z, \alpha).$$

Since $\int_0^\infty h(z, \alpha, g)\,dz = 1$, it follows that the birthrate m is equal to $m = 1/\int_0^\infty e^{-gz}F(z, \alpha)\,dz$. This yields equation (12.3). By definition, $m = \int_0^\infty h(z, \alpha, g)b(z)\,dz$, where $b(z)$ is the specific *fertility* rate at age z. Substituting the above definition of $h(z, \alpha, g)$, we obtain (12.4).

Aggregate steady-state savings per capita, S, are therefore

$$S = \int_0^\infty s^*(z, \alpha) h(z, \alpha, g) \, dz$$

$$= \int_0^{R^*} w(z) h(z, \alpha, g) \, dz - c^* \quad \text{from (12.6)}$$

$$= \int_0^{R^*} w(z) \left[\frac{e^{-gz}}{\int_0^\infty e^{-gz} F(z, \alpha) \, dz} - \frac{1}{\int_0^\infty F(z, \alpha) \, dz} \right] F(z, \alpha) \, dz. \quad (12.7)$$

It is seen that $S = 0$ when $g = 0$. A stationary economy without population growth has no aggregate savings per capita, corresponding to zero personal lifetime savings. We shall now show that $S > 0$ when $g > 0$. Denote average life expectancy of the population below a certain age, R, by $\tilde{z}(R)$. From (12.3),

$$\tilde{z}(R) = \int_0^R e^{-gz} z F(z, \alpha) \, dz \bigg/ \int_0^R e^{-gz} F(z, \alpha) \, dz. \quad (12.8)$$

The average population age, $\tilde{z}$, is

$$\tilde{z} = \tilde{z}(\infty) = \int_0^\infty e^{-gz} z F(z, \alpha) \, dz \bigg/ \int_0^\infty e^{-gz} F(z, \alpha) \, dz. \quad (12.9)$$

Clearly, $\tilde{z}(R) < \tilde{z}$ for any R.
Differentiating (12.7) partially with respect to g,

$$\frac{\partial S}{\partial g} = \left(\int_0^{R^*} e^{-gz} F(z, \alpha) \, dz \bigg/ \int_0^\infty e^{-gz} F(z, \alpha) \, dz \right) (\tilde{z} - \tilde{z}(R^*)) > 0. \quad (12.10)$$

A positive population growth rate, $g > 0$, entails positive aggregate steady-state savings.

To examine the effect of a change in α on aggregate savings, differentiate (12.7) totally,

$$\frac{dS}{d\alpha} = w(R^*) h(R^*, \alpha, g) \frac{dR^*}{d\alpha} - \frac{dc^*}{d\alpha} + \int_0^{R^*} w(z) \frac{dh(z, \alpha, g)}{d\alpha} \, dz. \quad (12.11)$$

Under the assumption that $\mu(z, \alpha)$ decreases with z, $dR^*/d\alpha < 0$ and $dc^*/d\alpha > 0$. Hence, when the last term in (12.11) is nonpositive, this ensures that $dS/d\alpha < 0$.

The sign of $dh(z, \alpha, g)/d\alpha$ reflects two opposite effects: An increase in longevity raises the survival function at all ages and, as shown above, also raises the population growth rate. By (12.3), the first effect raises h, while the second decreases it. Since

$$\int_0^\infty \frac{dh(z, \alpha, g)}{d\alpha} \, dz = 0, \qquad (12.12)$$

the crucial question is which of these effects is dominant at different ages. Since $w(z)$ is nonincreasing in z, it can be seen from (12.12) that the last term in (12.11) is negative when $dh/d\alpha$ is negative at small z and positive at large z. The interpretation is straightforward: A rise in longevity that raises the population steady-state density in "working ages" when individuals save and decreases the density in "retirement ages" when individuals dissave tends to increase aggregate savings (and *vice versa*). This is the age composition effect on aggregate savings.

Two additional assumptions are made to ensure that in steady state aggregate savings increase with longevity. First, it is assumed the age-specific birthrate, $b(z)$, does not increase with age:

$$b'(z) \le 0. \qquad (12.13)$$

Recall that $z = 0$ is the age when individuals plan for their future. So this is a natural assumption, certainly at the more advanced ages.

The second assumption is that *the elasticity of $\mu(z, \alpha)$ with respect to z does not exceed unity,*

$$\frac{z}{\mu(z, \alpha)} \frac{\partial \mu(z, \alpha)}{\partial z} \le 1, \quad \text{for all } z.\text{[2]} \qquad (12.14)$$

This assumption deserves an explanation.

Recall that in order to determine that individuals increase their lifetime expected savings as survival probabilities rise, it was assumed that improvements in longevity are tilted toward older ages, $\partial \mu(z, \alpha)/\partial z < 0$. Taken by itself, this implies that the increase in the population's density function is proportionately higher at older ages. Higher longevity also raises the population's steady-state growth rate. As seen in (12.3), this leads to a steeper rate of decline in the population density function with age. The above assumption, constraining the rate of increase of survival probabilities with age, ensures that between these two opposing effects the latter dominates.

---

[2] Note that the limiting case that satisfies this assumption is the exponential function, $F(z, \alpha) = e^{-\alpha z}$, $0 \le z \le \infty$, where $(z/\mu)(\partial \mu/\partial z) = 1$.

We can now state: *Under assumptions (12.13) and (12.14), aggregate steady-state savings rise with longevity, $dS/d\alpha < 0$.*

The proof is in the appendix to this chapter.

Note that the assumptions underlying this result are *sufficient* conditions, and hence a positive relation between longevity and aggregate savings may be empirically observed even when some of these assumptions are not satisfied. These assumptions are important, however, for empirical work because they provide specific hypotheses about the changes in survival probabilities that lead to a predictable response by individuals, that is, to a certain direction of the behavioral effect. For example, the common use of life expectancy as the explanatory variable for the level of savings is clearly inadequate and may even be misleading.

12.4 EXAMPLE: EXPONENTIAL SURVIVAL FUNCTION

The above expressions can be solved explicitly for the particular survival function $F(z, \alpha) = e^{-\alpha z}$, $z \geq 0$, a constant wage rate, $w(z) = w$, and a constant age-specific birthrate, $b(z) = b$.

Equation (12.11) becomes

$$c^* = w(1 - e^{-\alpha R^*}), \tag{12.15}$$

and from (12.1) and (12.2),

$$\frac{\alpha}{R^*} \frac{dR^*}{d\alpha} = -\frac{\sigma}{\sigma + \dfrac{R^* e'(R^*)}{e(R^*)} \left(\dfrac{e^{\alpha R^*} - 1}{\alpha R^*} \right)}, \tag{12.16}$$

$$\frac{\alpha}{c^*} \frac{dc^*}{d\alpha} = \frac{\alpha R^*}{e^{\alpha R^*} - 1} \left(1 + \frac{\alpha}{R^*} \frac{dR^*}{d\alpha} \right), \tag{12.17}$$

where $\sigma = -u''(c^*)c^*/u'(c^*)$.

Clearly,

$$1 \leq \frac{\alpha}{R^*} \frac{dR^*}{d\alpha} \leq 0 \quad \text{and} \quad 0 \leq \frac{\alpha}{c^*} \frac{dc^*}{d\alpha} \leq 1.$$

The steady-state age density function, (12.3), is

$$h(z, \alpha, g) = (g + \alpha)e^{-(g+\alpha)z} \tag{12.18}$$

The population growth rate, g, with a constant birthrate, b, is solved from (12.4), $g = b - \alpha$. Hence, $dg/d\alpha = -1$.

Aggregate steady-state savings, (12.7), are

$$S = e^{-\alpha R^*}(1 - e^{-gR^*}). \tag{12.19}$$

Totally differentiating (12.16),

$$\frac{dS}{d\alpha} = -we^{-\alpha R^*}\left\{1 + \frac{\alpha}{R^*}\frac{dR^*}{d\alpha}\left[1 - \frac{be^{-gR^*}}{\alpha}\right]\right\} < 0. \tag{12.20}$$

12.5 No Annuities

It was assumed that annuitization is available at all ages, which means that individuals can take full advantage of risk pooling. To demonstrate that this is a critical assumption, consider the case of no insurance.[3] The budget constraint now becomes

$$\int_0^\infty c(z)\,dz - \int_0^R w(z)\,dz = 0. \tag{12.21}$$

In the absence of insurance, there is also a constraint that assets must be non-negative at all ages (individuals cannot die with debt). Equating expected marginal utility across ages yields decreasing optimum consumption whose shape reflects the individual's degree of risk aversion. To demonstrate that the effects of a change in longevity on savings and retirement are, in general, indeterminate, it suffices to take particular utility and survival functions. Thus, assume that $u(c) = \ln c$ and $F(z, \alpha) = e^{-\alpha z}$. For a constant wage $w(z) = w$, optimum consumption, $\hat{c}(z)$, now becomes (instead of (12.1))

$$\hat{c}(z) = w\alpha\hat{R}e^{-\alpha z}. \tag{12.22}$$

Accordingly, individual savings, (12.6), are now

$$\hat{s}(z) = \begin{cases} w(1 - \alpha\hat{R}\,e^{-\alpha z}), & 0 \le z \le \hat{R}, \\ -w\alpha\hat{R}\,e^{-\alpha z}, & \hat{R} \le z \le \infty, \end{cases} \tag{12.23}$$

and optimum retirement is obtained from condition (12.2):

$$\frac{1}{\alpha\hat{R}}e^{\alpha\hat{R}} = e(\hat{R}). \tag{12.24}$$

[3] Social security systems provide such annuitization. Mandatory uniform formulas may, however, be inadequate for some individuals and excessive for others. See Sheshinski (2003, pp. 27–54).

For this condition to have a unique solution it is assumed that the left hand side of (12.20) strictly decreases with $\hat{R}$. This holds if and only if $\hat{R} < 1/\alpha$, i.e. optimum retirement age is lower than expected lifetime, which is reasonable. When this condition holds, then $d\hat{R}/d\alpha \leq 0$; that is, as before, an increase in longevity leads to an increase in retirement age.[4]

Aggregate steady-state savings, (12.7), now become

$$S = w \left[1 - e^{-(g+\alpha)\hat{R}} - \frac{\alpha \hat{R}(g + \alpha)}{g + 2\alpha} \right]. \qquad (12.25)$$

Taking into account that $dg/d\alpha = -1$, it is seen that, holding $\hat{R}$ constant, a decrease in α affects S positively. However, when the change in $\hat{R}$ is also taken into account, the direction of the change in S is indeterminate, depending on parameter configuration.

12.6 Unintended Bequests

The analysis in the previous section disregards the fact that in the absence of full annuitization there are *unintended bequests* that affect individual behavior and, in particular, individual savings. The empirical importance of bequests and intergenerational transfers is debated extensively. Among the inconclusive issues is the separation of planned bequests from those due to lack of annuity markets. See, for example, Kotlikoff and Summers (1981) and, recently, Kopczuk and Lupton (2005). A general equilibrium analysis of longevity effects on aggregate savings has to take these intergenerational transfers into account.

In the absence of full annuitization, uncertain lifetime generates a distribution of bequests that depends on survival probabilities. A proper comparison of steady states with and without annuitization requires derivation of the *ergodic, long-term, distribution of bequests* which, in turn, generates a distribution of individual and aggregate savings. A general analysis of this process is beyond the scope of this book. The issue can, however, be clarified by means of a simple example.

Suppose that individuals live one period and with probability p, $0 \leq p \leq 1$, two periods. With no time preference, expected lifetime utility, V, is

$$V = u(c) + pu(c_1), \qquad (12.26)$$

---

[4] The same condition ensures the non-negativity of assets at all ages ($S^*(0) = w(1 - \alpha R^*) > 0$).

where c is first-period consumption and c_1 is second-period consumption. Without annuities and a zero interest rate, the budget constraint is

$$c + c_1 = w + b, \tag{12.27}$$

where $w > 0$ is income and $b \geq 0$ is initial endowment. Let $u(c) = \ln c$. Then optimum consumption, $\hat{c}$ and $\hat{c}_1$, is

$$\hat{c}(b) = \frac{w + b}{1 + p}, \qquad \hat{c}_1(b) = \frac{p(w + b)}{1 + p}. \tag{12.28}$$

Having no bequest motive, individuals who live two periods leave no bequests. Consequently, some individuals will have no initial endowments. Others will have positive endowments that depend on the history of parental survival. In fact, the steady-state distribution of initial endowments is a *renewal process*.

Denote by $\hat{b}_k$ the initial endowment of an individual whose k previous generations of parents lived only one period. If p_0 is the probability of a zero endowment, then the probability of $\hat{b}_k$ is $(1 - p)^k \, p_0$. Since $p_0 \sum_{k=0}^{\infty} (1 - p)^k = 1$, it follows that $p_0 = p$. We can calculate $\hat{b}_k$ from (12.27):

$$\hat{b}_k = w + \hat{b}_{k-1} - \hat{c}(\hat{b}_{k-1}) = \left[\frac{p}{1+p} + \left(\frac{p}{1+p} \right)^2 + \cdots + \left(\frac{p}{1+p} \right)^k \right] w$$

$$= p \left(1 - \left(\frac{p}{1+p} \right)^{k-1} \right) \qquad k = 1, 2, \ldots. \tag{12.29}$$

Thus, the savings of an individual with endowment $\hat{b}_k$, $s(\hat{b}_k)$, are

$$s(\hat{b}_k) = w - \hat{c}(\hat{b}_k) = \left(\frac{p}{1+p} \right)^{k+1} w, \tag{12.30}$$

and expected total savings, S, are

$$S = p \sum_{k=1}^{\infty} s(\hat{b}_k)(1 - p)^k = \frac{p^2}{1+p} \sum_{k=1}^{\infty} \left(\frac{p(1 - p)}{1+p} \right)^k. \tag{12.31}$$

While $S > 0$ for any $0 < p < 1$, the sign of the effect on S of an increase in the survival probability p is indeterminate.

Incorporating a positive birthrate would not change this conclusion: *In the absence of a competitive annuity market, the effect of increased longevity on steady-state aggregate savings is indeterminate.*

Appendix

From (12.3),

$$\frac{dh(z,\alpha,g)/d\alpha}{h(z,\alpha,g)} = \frac{1}{m}\frac{dm}{d\alpha} - h(z,\alpha,g)z\frac{dg}{d\alpha} + h(z,\alpha,g)\mu(z,\alpha). \quad (12A.1)$$

Since $m = 1 \Big/ \int_0^\infty e^{-gz}F(z,\alpha)\,dz$,

$$\frac{1}{m}\frac{dm}{d\alpha} = \left(\int_0^\infty h(z,\alpha,g)z\,dz\right)\frac{dg}{d\alpha} - \int_0^\infty h(z,\alpha,g)\mu(z,\alpha)\,dz \quad (12A.2)$$

Substituting from (17), (12A.2) can be rewritten

$$\frac{1}{m}\frac{dm}{d\alpha} = A\int_0^\infty b(z)\varphi(z,\alpha,g)\,dz, \quad (12A.3)$$

where

$$A = \frac{\left(\int_0^\infty h(z,\alpha,g)z\,dz\right)\left(\int_0^\infty h(z,\alpha,g)\mu(z,\alpha)\,dz\right)}{\int_0^\infty h(z,\alpha,g)zb(z)\,dz} < 0 \quad (12A.4)$$

and

$$\varphi(z,\alpha,g) = \frac{h(z,\alpha,g)\mu(z,\alpha)}{\int_0^\infty h(z,\alpha,g)\mu(z,\alpha)\,dz} - \frac{h(z,\alpha,g)z}{\int_0^\infty h(z,\alpha,g)z\,dz} \quad (12A.5)$$

Since $\int_0^\infty \varphi(z,\alpha,g)\,dz = 0$, φ changes sign at least once, say at $z = \tilde{z}$. At this point, by (12A.5),

$$\frac{\mu(\tilde{z},\alpha)}{\int_0^\infty h(z,\alpha,g)\mu(z,\alpha)\,dz} = \frac{\tilde{z}}{\int_0^\infty h(z,\alpha,g)z\,dz} \quad (12A.6)$$

Differentiating φ with respect to z at $\tilde{z}$,

$$\varphi'(\tilde{z},\alpha,g) = \frac{\partial\mu(\tilde{z},\alpha)/\partial z}{\int_0^\infty h(z,\alpha,g)\mu(z,\alpha)\,dz} - \frac{1}{\int_0^\infty h(z,\alpha,g)z\,dz}$$

inserting from (12A.6)

$$= \frac{\mu(\tilde{z},\alpha)}{\tilde{z}\int_0^\infty h(z,\alpha,g)\mu(z,\alpha)\,dz}\left(\frac{\tilde{z}}{\mu(\tilde{z},\alpha)}\frac{\partial\mu(\tilde{z},\alpha)}{\partial z} - 1\right). \quad (12A.7)$$

By assumption (12.14)

$$\frac{z}{\mu(\tilde{z}, \alpha)} \frac{\partial \mu(z, \alpha)}{\partial z} \leq 1$$

implying that

$$\varphi'(\tilde{z}, \alpha, g) \leq 0. \tag{12A.8}$$

With strict inequality, (12A.8) implies that $\tilde{z}$ is unique and that

$$\varphi(\tilde{z}, \alpha, g) \gtreqless 0 \quad \text{as} \quad z \lesseqgtr \tilde{z}. \tag{12A.9}$$

Since $b'(z) \leq 0$, it follows from (12A.9) that

$$\int_0^\infty b(z)\varphi(z, \alpha, g)\, dz \geq b(\tilde{z}) \int_0^\infty \varphi(z, \alpha, g)\, dz = 0. \tag{12A.10}$$

In view of (12A.3), we conclude that $(1/m)(dm/d\alpha) \leq 0$.
Since

$$\int_0^\infty \frac{dh(z, \alpha, g)}{d\alpha}\, dz = 0,$$

$dh/d\alpha$ is either 0 for all z or changes sign at least once, say at $\hat{z}$. From (12A.1), at $\hat{z}$,

$$\frac{1}{m}\frac{dm}{d\alpha} - h(\hat{z}, \alpha, g)(\hat{z}\frac{dg}{d\alpha} - \mu(\hat{z}, \alpha)) = 0. \tag{12A.11}$$

Since $(1/m)(dm/d\alpha) \leq 0$, it follows that

$$\hat{z}\frac{dg}{d\alpha} - \mu(\hat{z}, \alpha) \leq 0. \tag{12A.12}$$

Partially differentiating $h(z, \alpha, g)$ with respect to z at $\hat{z}$ gives, by (12A.1),

$$\frac{\partial}{\partial z}\left(\frac{dh(\hat{z}, \alpha, g)}{d\alpha}\right) = -h(\hat{z}, \alpha, g)\left(\frac{dg}{d\alpha} - \frac{\partial \mu(\hat{z}, \alpha, g)}{\partial z}\right) \tag{12A.13}$$

From (12A.12) and the above assumption,

$$\geq -\frac{h(\hat{z}, \alpha, g)\mu(\hat{z}, \alpha)}{\hat{z}}\left(1 - \frac{\hat{z}}{\mu(\hat{z}, \alpha)} \frac{\partial \mu(\hat{z}, \alpha)}{\partial z}\right) \geq 0. \tag{12A.14}$$

Hence, unless $dh/d\alpha = 0$ for all z, $\hat{z}$ is unique and

$$\frac{dh(z, \alpha, g)}{d\alpha} \lesseqqgtr 0 \quad \text{as} \quad z \lesseqqgtr \hat{z}. \tag{12A.15}$$

Since $w(z)$ is non-increasing and

$$\int_0^\infty \frac{dh(z, \alpha, g)}{d\alpha} \, dz = 0,$$

it now follows from (A.15) that for any R^*,

$$\int_0^{R^*} w(z) \frac{dh(z, \alpha, g)}{d\alpha} \, dz < w(\hat{z}) \int_0^\infty \frac{dh(z, \alpha, g)}{d\alpha} \, dz = 0. \tag{12A.16}$$

By (12.11) and (12A.16), $dS/d\alpha < 0 \, \|$.

CHAPTER 13

Utilitarian Pricing of Annuities

13.1 FIRST-BEST ALLOCATION

We have seen in previous chapters that when annuity issuers can identify individuals' survival probabilities (*risk classes*), then annuity prices in competitive equilibrium (with a zero discount rate) are equal to these probabilities. That is, prices are *actuarially fair*. In contrast, the pricing implicit in social security systems invariably allows for cross-subsidization between different risk classes, implying transfers from high-to low-risk individuals. For example, most social security systems provide the same benefits to males and females of equal age who have equal income and retirement histories inspite of the higher life expectancy of females.[1] We now want to examine the utilitarian approach to this issue using the theory of optimum commodity taxation.

Consider a population that consists of H individuals. Denote the expected utility of individual h by V_h, $h = 1, 2, \ldots, H$. Utilitarianism attempts to maximize a social welfare function, W, which depends on the V_h values:

$$W = W(V_1, V_2, \ldots, V_H). \tag{13.1}$$

W depends positively on, and is assumed to be differentiable, symmetric, and concave in, the V_h's.

Each individual lives for either one or two periods, and individuals differ in their survival probabilities. Let p_h be the probability that individual h lives for two periods; let c_{1h} be the consumption of individual h in period 1 and c_{2h} be the consumption of individual h in period 2 if he or she is then alive. Utility derived from consumption, $c(>0)$, by any individual in any period during life is $u(c)(>0)$. It is the same in either period, so there is no *time preference*. When an individual is not alive, utility is 0. Expected utility of individual h is thus

$$V_h = u(c_{1h}) + p_h u(c_{2h}). \tag{13.2}$$

The economy has a given amount of resources, R, that can be used in either period, and they can be carried forward without any gain or loss.

---

[1] Further subsidization is provided when females are allowed to retire earlier. The best introduction to the broad theoretical issues discussed here is Diamond (2003).

With a large number of individuals, expected consumption in the two periods must therefore equal the given resources:

$$\sum_{h=1}^{H} c_{1h} + \sum_{h=1}^{H} p_h c_{2h} = R. \tag{13.3}$$

Maximization of (13.1) subject to (13.3) yields the condition that consumption is equal in both periods, $c_{1h} = c_{2h} = c_h$, for all $h = 1, 2, \ldots, H$. Consequently, expected utility, (13.2), becomes $V_h = (1 + p_h)u(c_h)$ and the resource constraint, (13.3), becomes

$$\sum_{h=1}^{H} (1 + p_h)c_h = R. \tag{13.4}$$

The first-best optimum allocation of consumption, c_h, among individuals is obtained by maximizing the welfare function, (13.1), subject to the resource constraint, (13.4). The first-order conditions are

$$W_h u'(c_h) = \text{constant}, \quad \text{for all } h = 1, 2, \ldots, H, \tag{13.5}$$

where $W_h = \partial W / \partial V_h$. Denote the solutions to (13.4) and (13.5) by $c_h^*(\mathbf{p})$, $\mathbf{p} = (p_1, p_2, \ldots, p_H)$, the corresponding optimum expected utilities by $V_h^* = (1 + p_h)u(c_h^*)$, and $W^* = W(V_1^*, V_2^*, \ldots V_n^*,)$.

It can be shown that for any $j, k = 1, 2, \ldots, H$, $V_j^* \gtreqless V_k^*$ as $p_j \gtreqless p_k$. To demonstrate this, take $H = 2$. Write the resource constraint (13.4) in terms of (V_1, V_2):

$$(1 + p_1)v \left(\frac{V_1}{1 + p_1} \right) + (1 + p_2)v \left(\frac{V_2}{1 + p_2} \right) = R, \tag{13.6}$$

where the function v is implicitly defined by $V_h = (1 + p_h)u(v)$. Hence, $v' > 0$ and $v'' < 0$. The implicit relation between V_1 and V_2 defined by (13.6) is strictly convex, and its absolute slope is equal to $v'(V_1/(1 + p_1))/v'(V_2/(1 + p_2))$. Hence, along the $V_1 = V_2$ line this slope is $\gtreqless 1$ as $p_1 \lesseqgtr p_2$ (figure 13.1). The symmetry of W implies that the slope of social indifference curves, $W_0 = W(V_1, V_2)$, along the 45-degree line is unity, and hence $V_1^* \gtreqless V_2^* \Longleftrightarrow p_1 \gtreqless p_2$.

The ranking of optimum consumption levels, $c_h^*(\mathbf{p})$, depends on more specific properties of the welfare and utility functions. For example, for an additive social welfare function, $W = \sum_{h=1}^{H} V_h$, (13.1)–(13.5) imply that

$$c_h^* = \frac{R}{\sum_{h=1}^{H}(1 + p_h)},$$

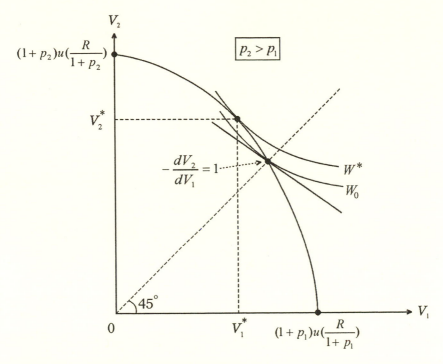

Figure 13.1. First-best allocation of utilities.

while

$$V_h^* = (1 + p_h) \, u \left(\frac{R}{\sum_{h=1}^{H} (1 + p_h)} \right).$$

Thus, the utilitarian first best has inequality in expected utilities but may have equality in consumption levels (Arrow, 1992).

This result is similar to Mirrlees' (1971) optimum income tax model where individuals differ in productivity.[2] The first best allocation provides higher (expected) utility to those with a higher capacity to produce utility.

In the appendix to this chapter it is shown that

$$0 > \frac{1 + p_n}{c_h^*} \frac{\partial c_h^*}{\partial p_h} > -1, \tag{13.7}$$

while $\partial c_h^* / \partial p_j \gtreqless 0$, for $j \neq h$, $h, j = 1, 2, \ldots, n$.

[2] In Mirrlees' model with additive utilities, the first best has all individuals with equal consumption, and those with higher productivity, having a lower disutility for generating a given income, are assigned to work more and hence have a lower utility.

Concavity of u and (13.7) imply

$$\frac{\partial V_h^*}{\partial p_h} = u(c_h^*) + (1 + p_n)u'(c_n)\frac{\partial c_h^*}{\partial p_n} > 0, \tag{13.8}$$

while $\partial V_h^*/\partial p_j \gtreqless 0$, $j \neq h$, $j = 1, 2, \ldots, H$.[3] Thus, with the given total resources, an increase in one individual's survival probability decreases his or her optimum consumption, but the positive effect of higher survival probability on expected utility dominates. The effect on the welfare of other individuals facing only resource redistribution depends on the shape of the social welfare function.

13.2 COMPETITIVE ANNUITY MARKET WITH FULL INFORMATION

In a competitive market with full information on the survival probabilities of individuals and a zero rate of interest, the price of a unit of second-period consumption, c_{2h}, is equal to the survival probability of each annuitant. Individuals maximize expected utility subject to a budget constraint

$$c_{1h} + p_h c_{2h} = y_h \qquad h = 1, 2, \ldots, H, \tag{13.9}$$

where y_h is the given income of individual h. Demands for first- and second-period consumption (annuities), $\hat{c}_{1h}$ and $\hat{c}_{2h}$, are given by $\hat{c}_{1h} = \hat{c}_{2h} = \hat{c}_h = y_h/(1 + p_h)$.

The first-best allocation can be supported by a competitive annuity market accompanied by an optimum income allocation. Equating consumption levels under competition, $\hat{c}_h$, to the optimum levels, $c_h^*(p)$, yields *unique* income levels, $\hat{y}_h = (1 + p_h)c_h^*(\mathbf{p})$, that support the *first-best* allocation. In particular, with an additive W, all individuals consume the same amount:

$$c_h^* = \frac{R}{\sum_{h=1}^{H}(1 + p_h)},$$

hence

$$\hat{y}_h = \frac{1 + p_h}{\sum_{h=1}^{H}(1 + p_h)}R. \tag{13.10}$$

---

[3] In the extreme case when $W = \min[V_1, V_2, \ldots, V_H]$, optimum expected utilities, $V_h^* = (1 + p_h)u(c_h^*)$, are equal, and hence optimum consumption, c_h^*, strictly decreases with p_h (and increases with p_j, $j \neq h$).

13.3 SECOND-BEST OPTIMUM PRICING OF ANNUITIES

Governments do not engage, for well-known reasons, in unconstrained lump-sum redistributions of incomes. In contrast, most annuities are supplied directly by government-run social security systems and taxes/subsidies can, if so desired, be applied to the prices of annuities offered by private pension funds. These prices can be used by governments to improve social welfare. Although deviations from actuarially fair prices entail distortions (i.e., efficiency losses), distributional improvements may outweigh the costs.[4]

Suppose that individual h purchases annuities at a price of q_h. With an income y_h, his or her budget constraint is

$$c_{1h} + q_h c_{2h} = y_h, \qquad h = 1, 2 \ldots, H. \tag{13.11}$$

Maximization of (13.2) subject to (13.11) yields demands $\widehat{c}_{ih} = \widehat{c}_{ih}(q_h, p_h, y_h)$, $i = 1, 2$, and $h = 1, 2, \ldots, H$. Maximized expected utility, $\widehat{V}_h$, is $\widehat{V}_h(q_h, p_h, y_h) = u(\widehat{c}_{1h}) + p_h u(\widehat{c}_{2h})$.

Assume that no outside resources are available for the annuity market, hence total subsidies/taxes must equal zero,

$$\sum_{h=1}^{H} (q_h - p_h)\widehat{c}_{2h} = 0. \tag{13.12}$$

Maximization of $W(\widehat{V}_1, \widehat{V}_2, \ldots, \widehat{V}_H)$ with respect to prices $(q_1, \ldots, q_H)$ subject to (13.12) yields the first-order condition

$$\frac{\partial W}{\partial \widehat{V}_h} \frac{\partial \widehat{V}_h}{\partial q_h} + \lambda \left[\widehat{c}_{2h} + (q_h - p_h)\frac{\partial \widehat{c}_{2h}}{dq_h} \right] = 0, \qquad h = 1, 2, \ldots, H, \tag{13.13}$$

where $\lambda > 0$ is the shadow price of constraint (13.12). In elasticity form, using Roy's identity $(\partial \widehat{V}_h/\partial q_h = -(\partial \widehat{V}_h/\partial y_h)\widehat{c}_{2h})$, (13.13) can be written

$$\frac{q_h - p_h}{q_h} = \frac{\theta_h}{\varepsilon_h}, \tag{13.14}$$

where $\varepsilon_h = -(q_h/\widehat{c}_{2h})(\partial \widehat{c}_{2h}/dq_h)$ is the *price elasticity* of second-period consumption of individual h and

$$\theta_h = 1 - \frac{1}{\lambda} \frac{\partial W}{\partial \widehat{V}_h} \frac{\partial \widehat{V}_h}{\partial y_h}$$

---

[4] In practice, of course, prices do not vary individually. Rather, individuals with similar survival probabilities are grouped into risk classes, and annuity prices and taxes/subsidies vary across these classes.

is the *net* social value of a marginal transfer to individual h through the optimum pricing scheme. Equation (13.14) is a variant of the well-known *inverse elasticity* optimum tax formula, which combines equity (θ_h) and efficiency $(1/\varepsilon_h)$ considerations.

The implication of (13.14) for the optimum pricing of annuities depends on the welfare function, W, and on the joint distribution of incomes, $(y_1, \ldots, y_H)$, and probabilities, $(p_1, \ldots, p_H)$.

To obtain some concrete examples, let W be the sum of expected utilities. Then $\partial W/\partial \widehat{V}_h = 1$, $h = 1, 2, \ldots, H$. Assume further that $V_h = \ln c_{1h} + p_h \ln c_{2h}$. In this case, demands are

$$\widehat{c}_{1h} = \frac{y_h}{1 + p_h}, \qquad \widehat{c}_{2h} = \frac{y_h}{1 + p_h}\frac{p_h}{q_h}, \qquad (13.15)$$

and

$$\widehat{V}_h = (1 + p_h)\ln\left(\frac{y_h}{1 + p_h}\right) + p_h \ln\left(\frac{p_h}{q_h}\right). \qquad (13.16)$$

Conditions (13.14) and (13.12) now yield the solution

$$q_h = \phi\left(\frac{\beta_h}{\sum_{h=1}^{H}\beta_h}\right), \qquad (13.17)$$

where

$$\phi = \sum_{h=1}^{H} p_h > 0 \quad \text{and} \quad \beta_h = \frac{p_h y_h}{1 + p_h} > 0.$$

Consider two special cases of (13.17):

(a) Equal incomes: $(y_h = y = R/H; \; h = 1, 2, \ldots, H)$

Condition (13.17) now becomes $q_h = \bar{\phi}\left(p_h/(1 + p_h)\right)$, where

$$\bar{\phi} = \frac{\sum_{h=1}^{H} p_h}{\sum_{h=1}^{H}\left(\dfrac{p_h}{1 + p_h}\right)} \quad (>1). \qquad (13.18)$$

It is seen (figure 13.2) that optimum pricing involves subsidization (taxation) of individuals with high (low) survival probabilities.[5]

---

[5] In figure 13.2, it can be shown that $\bar{\phi}/2 < 1$.

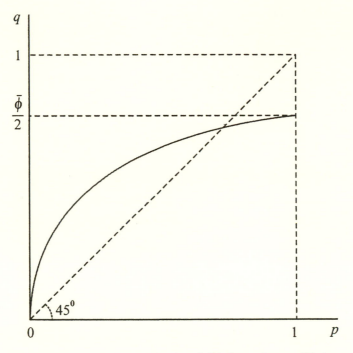

Figure 13.2. Optimum annuity pricing in a full-information equilibrium.

(b) $y_h = y(1 + p_h)$

This, one recalls, is the first-best utilitarian income distribution, and since all price elasticities are equal to unity, we see from (13.17), as expected, that $q_h = p_h$; that is efficiency prices are optimal.

More generally, it is seen from (13.17) that a higher correlation between incomes, y_h, and survival probabilities, p_h, decreases—and possibly eliminates—the subsidization of high-survival individuals. In contrast, a negative correlation between incomes and survival probabilities (as, presumably, in the female/male case) leads to subsidies for high- survival individuals, possibly to the commonly observed uniform pricing rule.

Appendix

Let $H = 2$. The extension to $H > 2$ is immediate. The first-order conditions for maximization of (13.1) subject to (13.3) are

$$W_1(U_1^*, U_2^*)u'(c_1^*) - \lambda = 0,$$

$$W_2(U_1^*, U_2^*)u'(c_2^*) - \lambda = 0,$$

$$R - (1 + p_1)c_1^* - (1 + p_2)c_2^* = 0, \qquad (13A.1)$$

where $U_h^* = (1 + p_h)u(c_h^*)$, $h = 1, 2$.

Totally differentiating (13A.1) with respect to p_1 yields

$$
\begin{aligned}
\frac{(1 + p_1)}{c_1^*}\frac{\partial c_1^*}{\partial p_1} = \frac{1}{\Delta}\Big\{ (1 + p_1)(1 + p_2)\Big[(W_{11}\,u'(c_1^*)^2 \\
- W_{12}\,u'(c_1^*)u'(c_2^*))\Big/ \frac{c_1^*u'(c_1^*)}{u(c_1^*)} - W_{12}\,u'(c_1^*)u'(c_2^*) \\
+ W_{22}\,u'(c_2^*)^2 \Big] + W_2 u''(c_2^*)(1 + p_1)\Big\},
\end{aligned}
\qquad (13A.2)
$$

where (using (13A.1))

$$
\begin{aligned}
\Delta = -\frac{(1 + p_1)(1 + p_2)\lambda^2}{W_1^2\,W_2^2}[W_{11}\,W_2^2 - 2\,W_{12}\,W_1\,W_2 + W_{22}\,W_1^2] \\
-(1 + p_1)\,W_2 u''(c_2^*) - (1 + p_2)\,W_1 u''(c_1^*).
\end{aligned}
\qquad (13A.3)
$$

Strict quasi-concavity of W implies that $\Delta > 0$.

Since $0 < c_1^* u'(c_1^*)/u(c_1^*) < 1$, inserting again (13A.1) into (13A.2), we obtain

$$0 > \frac{(1 + p_1^*)}{c_1^*}\frac{\partial c_1^*}{\partial p_1} > -1, \qquad (13A.4)$$

as stated in the text.

Differentiating (13A.1) with respect to p_2,

$$\frac{(1+p_2)}{c_2^*}\frac{\partial c_1^*}{\partial p_2} = \frac{1}{\Delta}\left\{(1+p_1)(1+p_2)\left[W_{11}\,u'(c_1^*)^2 - W_{22}\,u'(c_2^*)^2\left(\frac{u(c_2^*)}{c_2^*u'(c_2^*)}\right)\right.\right.$$

$$\left.\left. - W_{12}\,u'(c_1^*)u(c_2^*) - W_{12}\,u'(c_1^*)u(c_2^*)\left(\frac{u(c_2^*)}{c_2^*u'(c_2^*)}\right) - W_1\,u''(c_1^*)\right\}.$$

$$(13A.5)$$

The first term on the right hand side is negative, and the second is positive, hence the sign of $\partial c_1^*/\partial p_2$ cannot be established in general.

CHAPTER 14

Optimum Taxation in Pooling Equilibria

14.1 INTRODUCTION

We have argued that annuity markets are characterized by *asymmetric information* about the longevities of individuals. Consequently, annuities are offered at the same price to all potential buyers, leading to a pooling equilibrium. In contrast, the setting for the standard theory of optimum commodity taxation (Ramsey, 1927; Diamond and Mirrlees, 1971; Salanie, 2003) is a competitive equilibrium that attains an efficient resource allocation. In the absence of lump-sum taxes, the government wishes to raise revenue by means of distortive commodity taxes, and the theory develops the conditions that have to hold for these taxes to minimize the deadweight loss (*Ramsey–Boiteux conditions*). The analysis was extended in some directions to allow for an initial inefficient allocation of resources. In such circumstances, aside from the need to raise revenue, taxes/subsidies may serve as means to improve welfare because of market inefficiencies. The rules for optimum commodity taxation, therefore, mix considerations of shifting an inefficient market equilibrium in a welfare-enhancing direction and the distortive effects of gaps between consumer and producer marginal valuations generated by commodity taxes.

In this chapter we explore the general structure of optimum taxation in pooling equilibria, with particular emphasis on annuity markets. There is asymmetric information between firms and consumers about "relevant" characteristics that affect the *costs* of firms, as well as consumer preferences. This is typical in the field of insurance. Expected costs of medical insurance, for example, depend on the health characteristics of the insured. Of course, the value of such insurance to the purchaser depends on the same characteristics. Similarly, the costs of an annuity depend on the expected payout, which in turn depends on the individual's survival prospects. Naturally, these prospects also affect the value of an annuity to the individual's expected lifetime utility. Other examples where personal characteristics affect costs are rental contracts (e.g., cars) and fixed-fee contracts for the use of certain facilities (clubs).

The modelling of preferences and of costs is general, allowing for any finite number of markets. We focus, though, only on efficiency aspects, disregarding distributional (equity) considerations.[1] We obtain surprisingly simple modified Ramsey-Boiteux conditions and explain the deviations from the standard model. Broadly, the additional terms that emerge reflect the fact that the initial producer price of each commodity deviates from each consumer's marginal costs, being equal to these costs only on average. Each levied specific tax affects all prices (termed a *general-equilibrium effect*), and, consequently, a small increase in a tax level affects the quantity-weighted gap between producer prices and individual marginal costs, the direction depending on the relation between demand elasticities and costs.

14.2 Equilibrium with Asymmetric Information

We shall now generalize the analysis in previous chapters of pooling equilibria in a single (annuity) market to an *n*-good setting with pooling equilibria in several or all markets.

Individuals consume n goods, X_i, $i = 1, 2, \ldots, n$, and a numeraire, Y. There are H individuals whose preferences are characterized by a linearly separable utility function, U,

$$U = u^h(\mathbf{x}^h, \alpha) + y^h, \quad h = 1, 2, \ldots, H, \tag{14.1}$$

where $\mathbf{x}^h = (x_1^h, x_2^h \ldots, x_n^h,)$, x_i^h is the quantity of good i, and y^h is the quantity of the numeraire consumed by individual h. The utility function, u^h, is assumed to be strictly concave and differentiable in $\mathbf{x}^h$. Linear separability is assumed to eliminate distributional considerations, focusing on the efficiency aspects of optimum taxation. It is well known how to incorporate equity issues in the analysis of commodity taxation (e.g., Salanie, 2003).

The parameter α is a personal attribute that is singled out because it has *cost effects*. Specifically, it is assumed that the unit costs of good i consumed by individuals with a given α (type α) is $c_i(\alpha)$. Health and longevity insurance are leading examples of this situation. The health status of an individual affects both his consumption preferences and the costs to the medical insurance provider. Similarly, as discussed extensively in previous chapters, the payout of annuities (e.g., retirement benefits) is contingent on survival and hence depends on the individual's relevant mortality function. Other examples are car rentals and car insurance,

---

[1] We have a good idea how exogenous income heterogeneity can be incorporated in the analysis (e.g., Salanie, 2003).

whose costs and value to consumers depend on driving patterns and other personal characteristics.[2]

It is assumed that α is continuously distributed in the population, with a distribution function, $G(\alpha)$, over a finite interval, $\underline{\alpha} \leq \alpha \leq \bar{\alpha}$.

The economy has given total resources, $R > 0$. With a unit cost of 1 for the numeraire, Y, the aggregate resource constraint is written

$$\int_{\underline{\alpha}}^{\bar{\alpha}} [\mathbf{c}(\alpha)\mathbf{x}(\alpha) + y(\alpha)] \, dG(\alpha) = R, \tag{14.2}$$

where $\mathbf{c}(\alpha) = (c_1(\alpha), c_2(\alpha), \ldots, c_n(\alpha))$, $\mathbf{x}(\alpha) = (x_1(\alpha), x_2(\alpha), \ldots, x_n(\alpha))$, $x_i(\alpha)$ being the aggregate quantity of X_i consumed by all type α individuals: $x_i(\alpha) = \sum_{h=1}^{H} x_i^h(\alpha)$ and, correspondingly, $y(\alpha) = \sum_{h=1}^{H} y^h(\alpha)$.

The first-best allocation is obtained by maximization of a utilitarian welfare function, W:

$$W = \int_{\underline{\alpha}}^{\bar{\alpha}} \left[\sum_{h=1}^{H} (u^h(\mathbf{x}^h; \alpha) + y^h) \right] dG(\alpha), \tag{14.3}$$

subject to the resource constraint (14.2). The first-order condition for an interior solution equates marginal utilities and costs for all individuals of the same type. That is, for each α,

$$u_i^h(\mathbf{x}^h; \alpha) - c_i(\alpha) = 0, \quad i = 1, 2, \ldots, n; \quad h = 1, 2, \ldots, H, \tag{14.4}$$

where $u_i^h = \partial u^h / \partial x_i$. The unique solution to (14.4), denoted $\mathbf{x}^{*h}(\alpha) = (x_1^{*h}(\alpha), x_2^{*h}(\alpha), \ldots, x_n^{*h}(\alpha))$, and the corresponding total consumption of type α individuals $\mathbf{x}^*(\alpha) = (x_1^*(\alpha), x_2^*(\alpha) \ldots, x_n^*(\alpha))$, $x_i^*(\alpha) = \sum_{h=1}^{H} x_i^h(\alpha)$. Individuals' optimum level of the numeraire Y (and hence utility levels) is indeterminate, but the total amount, y^*, is determined by the resource constraint, $y^* = R - \int_{\underline{\alpha}}^{\bar{\alpha}} \mathbf{c}(\alpha)\mathbf{x}^*(\alpha) \, dG(\alpha)$.

The first-best allocation can be supported by competitive markets with individualized prices equal to marginal costs.[3] That is, if p_i is the price of good i, then efficiency is attained when all type α individuals face the same price, $p_i(\alpha) = c_i(\alpha)$.

When α is *private information* unknown to suppliers (and not verifiable by monitoring individuals' purchases), then for each good firms charge the same price to all individuals. This is called a (second-best) *pooling equilibrium*.

---

[2] Representation of these characteristics by a single parameter is, of course, a simplification.

[3] The only constraint on the allocation of incomes, $m^h(\alpha)$, is that they support an interior solution. The modifications required to allow for zero equilibrium quantities are well known and immaterial for the following.

Good X_i is offered at a price p_i to all individuals, $i = 1, 2, \ldots, n$. The competitive price of the numeraire is 1. Individuals maximize utility, (14.1), subject to the budget constraint

$$\mathbf{p}\mathbf{x}^h + y^h = m^h \qquad h = 1, 2, \ldots, H, \tag{14.5}$$

where $m^h = m^h(\alpha)$ is the (given) income of the hth type α individual. It is assumed that for all α, the level of m^h yields interior solutions. The first-order conditions are

$$u_i^h(\mathbf{x}^h; \alpha) - p_i = 0, \quad i = 1, 2, \ldots, n, \quad h = 1, 2, \ldots, H, \tag{14.6}$$

the unique solutions to (14.6) are the *compensated demand functions* $\hat{\mathbf{x}}^h(\mathbf{p}; \alpha) = \left(\hat{x}_1^h(\mathbf{p}; \alpha), \hat{x}_2^h(\mathbf{p}; \alpha), \ldots, \hat{x}_n^h(\mathbf{p}; \alpha)\right)$, and the corresponding type α total demands $\hat{\mathbf{x}}(\mathbf{p}; \alpha) = \sum_{h=1}^H \hat{\mathbf{x}}^h(\mathbf{p}; \alpha)$. The optimum levels of Y, $\hat{y}^h$, are obtained from the budget constraints (14.5): $\hat{y}^h(\mathbf{p}; \alpha) = m^h(\alpha) - \mathbf{p}\hat{\mathbf{x}}^h(\mathbf{p}; \alpha)$, with a total consumption of $\hat{y}(\mathbf{p}; \alpha) = \sum_{h=1}^H \hat{y}^h = \sum_{h=1}^H m^h(\alpha) - \mathbf{p}\hat{\mathbf{x}}(\mathbf{p}; \alpha)$. The economy is closed by the identity $R = \sum_{h=1}^H m^h(\alpha)$.

Let $\pi_i(\mathbf{p})$ be total profits in the production of good i:

$$\pi_i(\mathbf{p}) = p_i \hat{x}_i(\mathbf{p}) - \int_{\underline{\alpha}}^{\bar{\alpha}} c_i(\alpha) \hat{x}_i(\mathbf{p}; \alpha) \, dG(\alpha), \tag{14.7}$$

where $\hat{x}_i(\mathbf{p}) = \int_{\underline{\alpha}}^{\bar{\alpha}} \hat{x}_i(\mathbf{p}; \alpha) \, dF(\alpha)$ is the *aggregate demand* for good i.

A pooling equilibrium is a vector of prices, $\hat{\mathbf{p}}$, that satisfies $\pi_i(\hat{\mathbf{p}}) = 0$, $i = 1, 2, \ldots, n$, or[4]

$$\hat{p}_i = \frac{\int_{\underline{\alpha}}^{\bar{\alpha}} c_i(\alpha) \hat{x}_i(\hat{\mathbf{p}}; \alpha) \, dG(\alpha)}{\int_{\underline{\alpha}}^{\bar{\alpha}} \hat{x}_i(\hat{\mathbf{p}}; \alpha) \, dG(\alpha)}, \qquad i = 1, 2, \ldots, n. \tag{14.8}$$

Equilibrium prices are weighted averages of marginal costs, the weights being the equilibrium quantities purchased by the different α types. Writing (14.7) (or (14.8)) in matrix form,

$$\pi(\hat{\mathbf{p}}) = \hat{\mathbf{p}}X(\hat{\mathbf{p}}) - \int_{\underline{\alpha}}^{\bar{\alpha}} \mathbf{c}(\alpha) \hat{X}(\hat{\mathbf{p}}; \alpha) \, dG(\alpha) = 0, \tag{14.9}$$

where $\pi(\hat{\mathbf{p}}) = (\pi_1(\hat{\mathbf{p}}), \pi_2(\hat{\mathbf{p}}), \ldots, \pi_n(\hat{\mathbf{p}}))$,

$$\hat{X}(\hat{\mathbf{p}}; \alpha) = \begin{bmatrix} \hat{x}_1(\hat{\mathbf{p}}; \alpha) & & 0 \\ & \ddots & \\ 0 & & \hat{x}_n(\hat{\mathbf{p}}; \alpha) \end{bmatrix}, \tag{14.10}$$

---

[4] For general analyses of pooling equilibria see, for example, Laffont and Martimort (2002) and Salanie (1997). As before, we assume that only linear price policies are feasible.

$\hat{X}(\hat{\mathbf{p}}) = \int_{\underline{\alpha}}^{\bar{\alpha}} X(\hat{\mathbf{p}}; \alpha) \, dG(\alpha)$, $\mathbf{c}(\alpha) = (c_1(\alpha), c_2(\alpha), \ldots, c_n(\alpha))$, and $\mathbf{0}$ is the $1 \times n$ zero vector $\mathbf{0} = (0, 0, \ldots, 0)$. Let $\hat{K}(\hat{\mathbf{p}})$ be the $n \times n$ matrix with elements $\hat{k}_{ij}$,

$$\hat{k}_{ij}(\hat{\mathbf{p}}) = \int_{\underline{\alpha}}^{\bar{\alpha}} (\hat{p}_i - c_i(\alpha)) s_{ij}(\hat{\mathbf{p}}; \alpha) \, dG(\alpha), \qquad i, j = 1, 2, \ldots, n, \quad (14.11)$$

where $s_{ij}(\hat{\mathbf{p}}; \alpha) = \partial \hat{x}_i(\hat{\mathbf{p}}; \alpha)/\partial p_j$ are the substitution terms.

We know from general equilibrium theory that when $\hat{X}(p) + \hat{K}(p)$ is positive-definite for any $\mathbf{p}$, then there exist unique and globally stable prices, $\hat{\mathbf{p}}$, that satisfy (14.9). See the appendix to this chapter. We shall assume that this condition is satisfied. Note that when costs are independent of α, $\hat{p}_i - c_i = 0$, $i = 1, 2, \ldots, n$, $\hat{K} = 0$, and this condition is trivially satisfied.

14.3 Optimum Commodity Taxation

Suppose that the government wishes to impose specific commodity taxes on X_i, $i = 1, 2, \ldots, n$. Let the unit tax (subsidy) on X_i be t_i so that its (tax-inclusive) consumer price is $q_i = p_i + t_i$, $i = 1, 2, \ldots, n$. Consumer demands, $\hat{x}_i^h(\mathbf{q}; \alpha)$, are now functions of these prices, $\mathbf{q} = \mathbf{p} + \mathbf{t}$, $\mathbf{t} = (t_1, t_2, \ldots, t_n)$. Correspondingly, total demand for each good by type α individuals is $\hat{x}_i(\mathbf{q}; \alpha) = \sum_{h=1}^{H} \hat{x}_i^h(\mathbf{q}; \alpha)$.

As before, the equilibrium vector of consumer prices, $\hat{\mathbf{q}}$, is determined by zero-profits conditions:

$$\hat{q}_i = \frac{\int_{\underline{\alpha}}^{\bar{\alpha}} (c_i(\alpha) + t_i) \hat{x}_i(\hat{\mathbf{q}}; \alpha) \, dG(\alpha)}{\int_{\underline{\alpha}}^{\bar{\alpha}} \hat{x}_i(\hat{\mathbf{q}}; \alpha) \, dG(\alpha)}, \qquad i = 1, 2, \ldots, n, \quad (14.12)$$

or, in matrix form,

$$\pi(\hat{\mathbf{q}}) = \hat{\mathbf{q}}\hat{X}(\hat{\mathbf{q}}) - \int_{\underline{\alpha}}^{\bar{\alpha}} (\mathbf{c}(\alpha) + \mathbf{t}) \hat{X}(\hat{\mathbf{q}}; \alpha) \, dG(\alpha) = 0, \quad (14.13)$$

where $\hat{X}(\hat{\mathbf{q}}; \alpha)$ and $X(\hat{\mathbf{q}})$ are the diagonal $n \times n$ matrices defined above, with $\hat{\mathbf{q}}$ replacing $\hat{\mathbf{p}}$.

Note that each element in $\hat{K}(\hat{\mathbf{q}})$, $k_{ij}(\hat{\mathbf{q}}) = \int_{\underline{\alpha}}^{\bar{\alpha}} (\hat{p}_i - c_i(\alpha)) s_{ij}(\hat{\mathbf{q}}; \alpha) \, dG(\alpha)$, also depends on $\hat{p}_i$ or $\hat{q}_i - t_i$. It is assumed that $\hat{X}(\mathbf{q}) + \hat{K}(\mathbf{q})$ is positive-definite for all $\mathbf{q}$. Hence, given $\mathbf{t}$, there exist unique prices, $\hat{\mathbf{q}}$ (and the corresponding $\hat{\mathbf{p}} = \hat{\mathbf{q}} - \mathbf{t}$), that satisfy (14.13).

Observe that each equilibrium price, $\hat{q}_i$, depends on the whole vector of tax rates, $\mathbf{t}$. Specifically, differentiating (14.13) with respect to the tax rates, we obtain

$$(\hat{X}(\hat{q}) + \hat{K}(\hat{q}))\hat{Q} = \hat{X}(\hat{q}), \tag{14.14}$$

where $\hat{Q}$ is the $n \times n$ matrix whose elements are $\partial \hat{q}_i/\partial t_j$, $i, j = 1, 2, \ldots, n$.

All principal minors of $\hat{X} + \hat{K}$ are positive, and it has a well-defined inverse. Hence, from (14.14),

$$\hat{Q} = (\hat{X} + \hat{K})^{-1}\hat{X}. \tag{14.15}$$

It is seen from (14.15) that equilibrium consumer prices rise with respect to an increase in own tax rates:

$$\frac{\partial \hat{q}_i}{\partial t_i} = \hat{x}_i(\hat{q})\frac{|\hat{X} + \hat{K}|_{ii}}{|\hat{X} + \hat{K}|}, \tag{14.16}$$

where $|\hat{X} + \hat{K}|$ is the determinant of $\hat{X} + \hat{K}$ and $|\hat{X} + \hat{K}|_{ii}$ is the principal minor obtained by deleting the ith row and the ith column. In general, the sign of cross-price effects due to tax rate increases is indeterminate, depending on substitution and complementarity terms.

We also deduce from (14.15) that, as expected, $\hat{K} = 0$, $\partial \hat{q}_i/\partial t_i = 1$, and $\partial \hat{q}_i/\partial t_j = 0$, $i \neq j$, when costs in all markets are independent of customer type (no asymmetric information). That is, the initial equilibrium is efficient: $p_i - c_i = 0$, $i = 1, 2, \ldots, n$.

From (14.1) and (14.3), social welfare in the pooling equilibrium is written

$$W(\mathbf{t}) = \int_{\underline{\alpha}}^{\bar{\alpha}} \left[\sum_{h=1}^{H} u^h(\hat{\mathbf{x}}^h(\hat{\mathbf{q}}; \alpha)) - \mathbf{c}(\alpha)\hat{\mathbf{x}}(\hat{\mathbf{q}}; \alpha) \right] dG(\alpha) + R. \tag{14.17}$$

The problem of optimum commodity taxation can now be stated: The government wishes to raise a given amount, T, of tax revenue,

$$\mathbf{t}\hat{\mathbf{x}}(\hat{\mathbf{q}}) = T, \tag{14.18}$$

by means of unit taxes, $\mathbf{t} = (t_1, t_2, \ldots, t_n)$, that maximize $W(\mathbf{t})$.

Maximization of (14.17) subject to (14.18) and (14.15) yields, after substitution of $u_i^h - q_i = 0$, $i = 1, 2, \ldots, n$, $h = 1, 2, \ldots, H$ from the individual first-order conditions, that optimum tax levels, denoted $\hat{\mathbf{t}}$, satisfy,

$$(1 + \lambda)\hat{\mathbf{t}}\hat{S}\hat{Q} + \mathbf{1}\hat{K}\hat{Q} = -\lambda\mathbf{1}\hat{X}, \tag{14.19}$$

where $\hat{S}$ is the $n \times n$ aggregate substitution matrix whose elements are $s_{ij}(\hat{\mathbf{q}}) = \int_{\underline{\alpha}}^{\bar{\alpha}} s_{ij}(\hat{\mathbf{q}}; \alpha)\,dG(\alpha)$, $\mathbf{1}$ is the $1 \times n$ unit vector, $\mathbf{1} = (1, 1, \ldots, 1)$, and $\lambda > 0$ is the *Lagrange multiplier* of (14.18).

Rewrite (14.19) in the more familiar form:

$$\hat{t}S = -\frac{1}{1+\lambda}\left[1(\lambda\hat{X}+\hat{K}\hat{Q})\hat{Q}^{-1}\right],$$

and substituting from (14.15),

$$\hat{t}S = \frac{\lambda}{1+\lambda}1\hat{X} - 1\hat{K}. \tag{14.20}$$

Equation (14.20) is our fundamental result. Let's examine these optimality conditions with respect to a particular tax, t_i:

$$\sum_{j=1}^{n}\hat{t}_j s_{ji}(\hat{q}) = -\frac{\lambda}{1+\lambda}\hat{x}_i(\hat{q}) - \sum_{j=1}^{n}\hat{k}_{ji}. \tag{14.21}$$

Denoting aggregate demand elasticities by $\varepsilon_{ij} = \varepsilon_{ij}(q) = q_j s_{ij}(q)/\hat{x}_i(q)$, $i, j = 1, 2, \ldots, n$, and using symmetry, $s_{ij}(q) = s_{ji}(\hat{q})$, (14.21) can be rewritten in elasticity form:

$$\sum_{j=1}^{n}\hat{t}'_j \varepsilon_{ij}(\hat{q})_{ji}(\hat{q}) = -\theta - \sum_{j=1}^{n}\hat{k}'_{ji}, \tag{14.22}$$

where $\hat{t}'_j = \hat{t}_j/\hat{q}_j$, $j = 1, 2, \ldots, n$, are the optimum ratios of taxes to consumer prices, $\theta = \lambda/(1+\lambda)$,

$$\hat{k}'_{ji} = \frac{1}{\hat{q}_i\hat{x}_i(\hat{q})}\int_{\underline{\alpha}}^{\bar{\alpha}}(\hat{p}_j - c_j)\hat{x}_j(\hat{q};\alpha)\varepsilon_{ji}(\hat{q};\alpha)\,dG(\alpha), \tag{14.23}$$

and $\varepsilon_{ji}(\hat{q};\alpha) = \hat{q}_i s_{ji}(\hat{q};\alpha)/x_j(\hat{q};\alpha)$, $i, j = 1, 2, \ldots, n$, are demand elasticities.

Compared to the standard case, $\hat{k}_{ji} = \hat{k}'_{ji} = 0$, $i, j = 1, 2, \ldots, n$, the *modified Ramsey–Boiteux conditions*, (14.21) or (14.22), have the additional term, $\sum_{j=1}^{n}\hat{k}_{ji}$ or $\sum_{j=1}^{n}\hat{k}'_{ji}$, respectively, on the right hand side. The interpretation of this term is straightforward.

In a pooling equilibrium, prices are weighted averages of marginal costs, the weights being the equilibrium quantities, (14.9). Since demands, in general, depend on all prices, all equilibrium prices are interdependent. It follows that an increase in the unit tax of any good affects *all* equilibrium (producer and consumer) prices. This general-equilibrium effect of a specific tax is present also in perfectly competitive economies with nonlinear technologies, but these price effects have no first-order welfare effects because of the equality of prices and marginal costs. In contrast, in a pooling equilibrium, where prices deviate from marginal costs (being equal to the latter only on average), there is a first-order welfare implication. The term $\hat{k}_{ji} = \int_{\underline{\alpha}}^{\bar{\alpha}}(\hat{p}_j - c_j(\alpha))s_{ij}(\hat{q};\alpha)$ $\times\, dG(\alpha)$ (or the equivalent term $\hat{k}'_{ji}$) is a welfare loss (< 0) or gain (>0) equal to the difference between the producer price and the marginal costs of type α individuals, positive or negative, times the change in the quantity of good j due to an increase in the price of good i. As we shall show below, the sign of $\hat{k}_{ji}$ (or $\hat{k}'_{ji}$) depends on the relation between demand elasticity and α.

As seen from (14.21) or (14.22), the signs of $\sum_{j=1}^{n}\hat{k}_{ji}$ (respectively $\hat{k}'_{ji}$) $i = 1, 2, \ldots, n$ determine the direction in which optimum taxes in a pooling equilibrium differ from those taxes in an initially efficient equilibrium. It can be shown that the sign of these terms depends on the relation between demand elasticities and costs. Specifically, $\hat{k}'_{ji} > 0\ (< 0)$ when ε_{ji} increases (decreases) with α. (See the proof in appendix B.)

An implication of this result is that when all elasticities ε_{ji} are constant, then $\hat{k}'_{ji} = 0$, $i, j = 1, 2, \ldots, n$, (14.20) or (14.21) become the standard Ramsey–Boiteux conditions, solving for the *same* optimum tax structure.

The intuition for the above condition is the following: $\hat{k}_{ji} < 0$ means that profits of good j fall as q_i increases, calling for an increase in the equilibrium price of good j. This "negative" effect due to the pooling equilibrium leads, by (14.20), to a smaller tax on good i compared to the standard case. Of course, this conclusion holds only if this effect has the same sign when summing over all markets, $\sum_{j=1}^{n}k_{ji} < 0$. The opposite conclusion follows when $\sum_{j=1}^{n}k_{ji} > 0$.

14.4 Optimum Taxation of Annuities

Consider individuals who consume three goods: annuities, life insurance, and a numeraire. Each annuity pays \$1 to the holder as long as he lives. Each unit of life insurance pays \$1 upon the death of the policy owner. There is one representative individual, and for simplicity let expected utility, U, be separable and have no time preference:

$$U = u(a)z + v(b) + y, \qquad (14.24)$$

where a is the amount of annuities, z is expected lifetime, b is the amount of life insurance (=bequests), and y is the amount of the numeraire. Utility of consumption, u, and the utility from bequests, v, are assumed to be strictly concave. As before, we assume that the equilibrium values of all variables are strictly positive.

Individuals are differentiated by their survival prospects. Let α represent an individual's risk class (type α), $z = z(\alpha)$, z strictly decreasing in α.

Here α is taken to be continuously distributed in the population over the interval $\underline{\alpha} \le \alpha \le \bar{\alpha}$, with a distribution function, $G(\alpha)$. Accordingly, the average lifetime in the population is $\bar{z} = \int_{\underline{\alpha}}^{\bar{\alpha}} z(\alpha)\, dG(\alpha)$.

Assume a zero rate of interest. In a full-information competitive equilibrium, the price of an annuity for type α individuals is $z(\alpha)$, and the prices of life insurance and of the numeraire are 1. All individuals purchase the same amount of annuities and life insurance and, for a given income, optimum utility increases with life expectancy, $z(\alpha)$.

Let p_a and p_b be the prices of annuities and life insurance, respectively, in a pooling equilibrium. Individuals' budget constraints are

$$p_a a + p_b b + y = m. \tag{14.25}$$

The maximization of (14.24) subject to (14.25) yields (compensated) demand functions $\hat{a}(p_a, p_b; \alpha)$ and $\hat{b}(p_a, p_b; \alpha)$, while $\hat{y} = m - p_a\hat{a} - p_b\hat{b}$. Profits of the two goods, π_a and π_b, are

$$\pi_a(p_a, p_b) = \int_{\underline{\alpha}}^{\bar{\alpha}} (p_a - z(\alpha))\hat{a}(p_a, p_b; \alpha)\, dG(\alpha),$$

$$\pi_b(p_a, p_b) = \int \underline{\alpha}^{\bar{\alpha}} (p_b - 1)\hat{b}(p_a, p_b; \alpha)\, dG(\alpha). \tag{14.26}$$

Equilibrium prices, denoted $\hat{p}_a$ and $\hat{p}_b$, are implicitly determined by $\pi_a = \pi_b = 0$. Clearly, $\hat{p}_b = 1$ (since 1 is the unit cost for all individuals).

Aggregate quantities of annuities and life insurance are $\hat{a}(p_a, p_b) = \int_{\underline{\alpha}}^{\bar{\alpha}} \hat{a}(p_a, p_b; \alpha)\, dG(\alpha)$ and $\hat{b}(p_a, p_b) = \int_{\underline{\alpha}}^{\bar{\alpha}} \hat{b}(p_a, p_b; \alpha)\, dG(\alpha)$, respectively. We assume (see appendix) that

$$\hat{a}(p_a, p_b) + \hat{k}_{11} > 0, \qquad \hat{b}(p_a, p_b) + \hat{k}_{22} > 0,$$

and

$$\left(\hat{a}(p_a, p_b) + \hat{k}_{11}\right)\left(\hat{b}(p_a, p_b) + \hat{k}_{22}\right) - \hat{k}_{12}\hat{k}_{21} > 0, \tag{14.27}$$

where[5]

$$\hat{k}_{1i} = \int_{\underline{\alpha}}^{\bar{\alpha}} (p_a - z(\alpha))s_{1i}\, dG(\alpha), \qquad s_{1i} = \frac{\partial \hat{a}(p_a, p_b; \alpha)}{\partial p_i}, \qquad i = a, b,$$

and

$$\hat{k}_{2i} = \int_{\underline{\alpha}}^{\bar{\alpha}} (p_b - 1)s_{2i}\, dG(\alpha), \qquad s_{2i} = \frac{\partial \hat{b}(p_a, p_b; \alpha)}{\partial p_i}, \qquad i = a, b. \tag{14.28}$$

[5] By concavity and separability, (14.24), $s_{11} < 0$, $s_{22} < 0$, and $s_{12}, s_{21} > 0$.

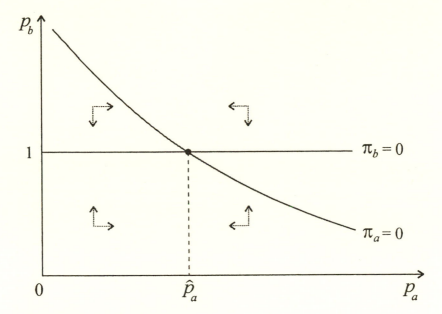

Figure 14.1. Unique pooling equilibrium.

As seen in figure 14.1 (drawn for the case $k_{12} > 0$), the pooling equilibrium $(\hat{p}_a, \hat{p}_b = 1)$ is unique and stable.

Now consider unit taxes, t_a and t_b, imposed on annuities and life insurance with consumer prices denoted $q_a = p_a + t_a$ and $q_b = p_b + t_b$, respectively. Applying the optimality conditions (14.21), optimum taxes, $(\hat{t}_a, \hat{t}_b)$, satisfy the conditions

$$s_{11}\hat{t}_a + s_{21}\hat{t}_b = -\theta\hat{a}(\hat{q}_a, \hat{q}_b) - \hat{k}_{11},$$
$$s_{12}\hat{t}_a + s_{22}\hat{t}_b = -\theta\hat{b}(\hat{q}_a, \hat{q}_b) - \hat{k}_{12} \tag{14.29}$$

where $0 < \theta < 1$, $s_{ij}(\hat{q}_a, \hat{q}_b) = \int_{\underline{\alpha}}^{\bar{\alpha}} s_{ij}(\hat{q}_a, \hat{q}_b; \alpha)\, dG(\alpha)$, $s_{1i}(\hat{q}_a, \hat{q}_b; \alpha) = \partial\hat{a}(\hat{q}_a, \hat{q}_b; \alpha)/\partial q_i$, $s_{2i}(\hat{q}_a, \hat{q}_b; \alpha) = \partial\hat{b}(\hat{q}_a, \hat{q}_b; \alpha)/\partial q_i$, $i = a, b$, and $\hat{k}_{11} = \int_{\underline{\alpha}}^{\bar{\alpha}} (\hat{p}_a - z(\alpha)) s_{11}(\hat{q}_a, \hat{q}_b; \alpha)\, dG(\alpha)$.

Equations (14.29) are the modified Ramsey–Boiteux conditions for the case of one pooling market.

To see in what direction the pooling equilibrium affects optimum taxes, write (14.29) in elasticity form, using symmetry $s_{ij} = s_{ji}$, $\varepsilon_{11} = \hat{q}_a s_{11}/\hat{a}$, $\varepsilon_{12} = \hat{q}_a s_{12}/\hat{a}$, $\varepsilon_{21} = \hat{q}_b s_{21}/\hat{b}$, $\varepsilon_{22} = \hat{q}_b s_{22}/\hat{b}$:

$$\varepsilon_{11}\hat{t}'_a + \varepsilon_{12}\hat{t}'_b = -\theta - \frac{\hat{k}'_{11}}{\hat{a}}, \quad \varepsilon_{21}\hat{t}'_a + \varepsilon_{22}\hat{t}'_b = -\theta - \frac{\hat{k}'_{12}}{\hat{b}} \tag{14.30}$$

where $\hat{t}'_a = \hat{t}_a/\hat{q}_a$ and $\hat{t}'_b = t_b/q_b$ are the ratios of optimum taxes to consumer prices. Solving (14.30) for the tax rates, using the identities $\varepsilon_{i0} + \varepsilon_{i1} + \varepsilon_{i2} = 0, i = 1, 2$, where 0 denotes the untaxed numeraire,

$$\frac{\hat{t}'_a}{\hat{t}'_b} = \frac{\varepsilon_{11} + \varepsilon_{22} + \varepsilon_{10} + \hat{k}'_{11}\varepsilon_{22}/\theta\hat{a} - \hat{k}_{12}\varepsilon_{12}/\theta\hat{b}}{\varepsilon_{11} + \varepsilon_{22} + \varepsilon_{20} + \hat{k}'_{12}\varepsilon_{11}/\theta\hat{b} - \hat{k}'_{11}\varepsilon_{21}/\theta\hat{a}}. \qquad (14.31)$$

We know that optimum tax ratios depend on complementarity or substitution of the taxed goods with the untaxed good, $\varepsilon_{i0}, i = 1, 2$. The additional terms, due to the pooling equilibrium in the annuity market, may be negative or positive. Consider the simple case $\hat{k}'_{12} = \varepsilon_{12} = \varepsilon_{21} = 0$ (no cross effects). We have shown that $\hat{k}'_{11} > 0$ when the elasticity of the demand for annuities decreases with life expectancy, $z(\alpha)$. Observe that a higher $z(\alpha)$ increases the amount of annuities purchased, $\partial\hat{a}/\partial\alpha > 0$. Hence, in this case, the additional term tends to (relatively) reduce the tax on annuities. The opposite argument applies when $\hat{k}'_{11} < 0$.

Appendix

A. Uniqueness and Stability

An interior pooling equilibrium, $\hat{\mathbf{p}}$, is defined by the system of equations

$$\pi(\hat{\mathbf{p}}) = \hat{\mathbf{p}}\hat{\mathbf{X}}(\hat{\mathbf{p}}) - \int_{\underline{\alpha}}^{\bar{\alpha}} \mathbf{c}(\alpha)\hat{\mathbf{X}}(\hat{\mathbf{p}};\alpha)\,dG(\alpha) = 0, \qquad (14A.1)$$

where $\pi(\hat{\mathbf{p}}) = (\pi_1(\hat{\mathbf{p}}), \pi_2(\hat{\mathbf{p}}), \ldots, \pi_n(\hat{\mathbf{p}}))$, $\hat{\mathbf{p}} = (\hat{p}_1, \hat{p}_2, \ldots, \hat{p}_n)$, $\hat{\mathbf{X}}(\hat{\mathbf{p}})$ is the diagonal $n \times n$ matrix,

$$\hat{\mathbf{X}}(\hat{\mathbf{p}}) = \begin{bmatrix} \hat{x}_1(\hat{\mathbf{p}}) & & 0 \\ & \ddots & \\ 0 & & \hat{x}_n(\hat{\mathbf{p}}) \end{bmatrix}, \qquad (14A.2)$$

while $X(\mathbf{p};\alpha)$ is the diagonal $n \times n$ matrix,

$$\hat{\mathbf{X}}(\hat{\mathbf{p}};\alpha) = \begin{bmatrix} \hat{x}_1(\hat{\mathbf{p}};\alpha) & & 0 \\ & \ddots & \\ 0 & & \hat{x}_n(\hat{\mathbf{p}};\alpha) \end{bmatrix}, \qquad (14A.3)$$

and $\mathbf{c}(\alpha) = (c_1(\alpha), c_2(\alpha), \ldots, c_n(\alpha))$.

It is well known from general equilibrium theory (Arrow and Hahn, 1971) that a sufficient condition for $\hat{\mathbf{p}}$ to be unique is that the $n \times n$ matrix $\hat{\mathbf{X}}(\hat{\mathbf{p}}) + \hat{K}(\hat{\mathbf{p}})$ be *positive-definite*, where $\hat{K}(\hat{\mathbf{p}})$ is the $n \times n$ matrix whose elements are $\hat{k}_{ij} = \int_{\underline{\alpha}}^{\bar{\alpha}}(\hat{p}_i - c_i(\alpha))s_{ij}(\hat{\mathbf{p}};\alpha)\,dG(\alpha)$, $s_{ij}(\hat{\mathbf{p}};\alpha) = \partial \hat{x}_i(\hat{\mathbf{p}};\alpha)/\partial p_j$, $i, j = 1, 2, \ldots, n$.

Furthermore, if the price of each good is postulated to change in a direction opposite to the sign of the profits of this good, then this condition also implies that price dynamics are globally stable, converging to the unique $\hat{\mathbf{p}}$.

Intuitively, as seen from (14A.1), an upward perturbation of p_1 raises π_1 if and only if $\hat{x}_1 + \int_{\underline{\alpha}}^{\bar{\alpha}}(\hat{p}_1 - c_1)s_{11}\,dG(\alpha) > 0$, leading to a decrease in p_1. A simultaneous upward perturbation of p_1 and p_2 raises π_1, and π_2 the 2×2 upper principal minor of Δ, is positive, and so on. Convexity of profit functions is the standard assumption in general equilibrium theory.

B. Sign of k_{ij}

Assume that $\varepsilon_{ji}(\hat{\mathbf{q}};\alpha) = \hat{q}_i s_{ji}(\mathbf{q};\alpha)/\hat{x}_j(\mathbf{q};\alpha)$ increases with α. Since in equilibrium

$$\int_{\underline{\alpha}}^{\bar{\alpha}} (\hat{p}_j - c_j(\alpha))\hat{x}_j(\hat{\mathbf{q}};\alpha)\, dG(\alpha) = 0 \tag{14B.1}$$

and, by assumption, $c_j(\alpha)$ increases with α, $\hat{p}_j - c_j(\alpha)$ changes sign once over $(\underline{\alpha}, \bar{\alpha})$, say at $\tilde{\alpha}$:

$$(\hat{p}_j - c_j(\alpha))\hat{x}_j(\hat{\mathbf{q}};\alpha) \gtreqless 0 \quad \text{as} \quad \alpha \lesseqgtr \tilde{\alpha}. \tag{14B.2}$$

Hence,

$$(\hat{p}_j - c_j(\alpha))s_{ji}(\hat{\mathbf{q}};\alpha) < \frac{\varepsilon_{ji}(\hat{\mathbf{q}};\tilde{\alpha})}{\hat{q}_i}(\hat{p}_j - c_j(\alpha))\hat{x}_j(\hat{\mathbf{q}};\alpha) \tag{14B.3}$$

for all $\alpha\varepsilon[\underline{\alpha}, \bar{\alpha}]$. Integrating on both sides of (14B.3), using (14B.1),

$$\int_{\underline{\alpha}}^{\bar{\alpha}} (\hat{p}_j - c_j(\alpha))s_{ji}(\alpha)\, dG(\alpha) < \frac{\varepsilon_{ji}(\hat{\mathbf{q}};\tilde{\alpha})}{\hat{q}_i} \int_{\underline{\alpha}}^{\bar{\alpha}} (\hat{p}_j - c_j(\alpha))\hat{x}_j(\hat{\mathbf{q}};\alpha)\, dG(\alpha) = 0. \tag{14B.4}$$

The inequality in (14B.4) is reversed when $\varepsilon_{ji}(\hat{\mathbf{q}};\alpha)$ decreases with α.

CHAPTER 15

Bundling of Annuities and Other Insurance Products

15.1 INTRODUCTION

It is well-known that monopolists who sell a number of products may find it profitable to "bundle" the sale of some of these products, that is, to sell "packages" of products with fixed quantity weights (see, for example, Pindyck and Rubinfeld (2007) pp. 404–414). In contrast, in perfectly competitive equilibria (with no increasing returns to scale or scope), such bundling is not sustainable. The reason is that if some products are bundled by one or more firms at prices that deviate from marginal costs, other firms will find it profitable to offer the bundled products separately, at prices equal to marginal costs, and consumers will choose to purchase the unbundled products in proportions that suit their preferences. This conclusion has to be modified under asymmetric information. We shall demonstrate below that competitive pooling equilibria may include bundled products. This is particularly relevant for the annuities market.

The reason for this outcome is that *bundling may reduce the extent of adverse selection* and, consequently, tends to reduce prices. In the terminology of the previous chapter, consider two products, X_1 and X_2, whose unit costs when sold to a type α individual are $c_1(\alpha)$ and $c_2(\alpha)$, respectively. Suppose that $c_1(\alpha)$ increases while $c_2(\alpha)$ decreases in α. Examples of particular interest are *annuities, life insurance,* and *health insurance.* The cost of an annuity rises with longevity. The cost of life insurance, on the other hand, typically depends negatively (under positive discounting) on longevity. Similarly, the costs of *medical care* are negatively correlated with health and longevity. Therefore, selling a package composed of annuities with life insurance or with health insurance policies tends to mitigate the effects of adverse selection because, when bundled, the negative correlation between the costs of these products reduces the overall variation of the costs of the bundle with individual attributes (health and longevity) compared to the variation of each product separately. This in turn is reflected in lower equilibrium prices.

Based on the histories of a sample of people who died in 1986, Murtaugh, Spillman, and Warshawsky (2001), simulated the costs of bundles of annuities and long-term care insurance (at ages 65 and 75) and found that the cost of the hypothetical bundle was lower by 3 to 5 percent compared to the cost of these products when purchased separately. They also found that bundling increases significantly the number of people who purchase the insurance, thereby reducing adverse selection. Bodie (2003) also suggested that bundling of annuities and long-term care would reduce costs for the elderly.

Currently, annuities and life insurance policies are jointly sold by many insurance companies though health insurance, at least in the United States, is sold by specialized firms (HMO$_s$). Consistent with the above studies, there is a discernible tendency in the insurance industry to offer plans that bundle these insurance products (e.g., by offering discounts to those who purchase jointly a number of insurance policies).

We have been told that in the United Kingdom there are insurance companies who bundle annuities and long-term medical care but could not find written references to this practice.

15.2 EXAMPLE

Let the utility of an type α individual be

$$u(x_1, x_2, y; \alpha) = \alpha \ln x_1 + (1 - \alpha) \ln x_2 + y, \qquad (15.1)$$

where x_1, x_2, and y are the quantities consumed of goods X_1 and X_2 and the numeraire, Y. It is assumed that α has a uniform distribution in the population over $[0, 1]$. Assume further that the unit costs of X_1 and X_2 when purchased by a type α individual are $c_1(\alpha) = \alpha$ and $c_2(\alpha) = 1 - \alpha$, respectively. The unit costs of Y are unity $(= 1)$.

Suppose that X_1 and X_2 are offered separately at prices p_1 and p_2, respectively. The individual's budget constraint is

$$p_1 x_1 + p_2 x_2 + y = R, \qquad (15.2)$$

where $R(>1)$ is given income.

Maximization of (15.1) subject to (15.2) yields demands $\hat{x}_1(p_1; \alpha) = \alpha/p_1$, $\hat{x}_2(p_2; \alpha) = (1 - \alpha)/p_2$ and $\hat{y} = R - 1$. The indirect utility, $\hat{u}$, is therefore

$$\hat{u}(p_1, p_2; \alpha) = \ln \left[\left(\frac{\alpha}{p_1} \right)^\alpha \left(\frac{1 - \alpha}{p_2} \right)^{1-\alpha} \right] + R - 1. \qquad (15.3)$$

As shown in previous chapters, the equilibrium pooling prices, $(\hat{p}_1, \hat{p}_2)$, are (for a uniform distribution of α)

$$\hat{p}_i = \frac{\int_0^1 c_i(\alpha)\hat{x}_i(\hat{p}_i; \alpha)\, d\alpha}{\int_0^1 \hat{x}_i(\hat{p}_i; \alpha)\, d\alpha} = \frac{2}{3} \qquad i = 1, 2. \tag{15.4}$$

Now suppose that X_1 and X_2 are sold jointly in equal amounts. Denote the respective amounts by x_1^b and x_2^b, $x_1^b = x_2^b$. Denote the price of the bundle by q. The budget constraint is now

$$q x_1^b + y^b = R. \tag{15.5}$$

Suppose that individuals purchase only bundles (we discuss this below). Maximization of (15.1), with $x_1^b = x_2^b$, subject to (15.5) yields demands $\hat{x}_1^b = 1/q$ and $\hat{y}^b = R - 1$. The equilibrium price of the bundle, $\hat{q}$, is

$$\hat{q} = \frac{\int_0^1 [c_1(\alpha) + c_2(\alpha)]\, \hat{x}_1^b(\hat{q}; \alpha)\, d\alpha}{\int_0^1 \hat{x}_1^b(\hat{q}; \alpha)\, d\alpha} = 1. \tag{15.6}$$

Thus, the level of the indirect utility of an individual who purchases the bundle, $\hat{u}^b$, is

$$\hat{u}^b = R - 1. \tag{15.7}$$

Comparing (15.3) with (15.7), we see that, with $\hat{p}_1 = \hat{p}_2 = \frac{2}{3}$, $\hat{u} \gtrless \hat{u}^b \Leftrightarrow \frac{3}{2}\alpha^\alpha(1 - \alpha)^{1-\alpha} \gtrless 1$, $\alpha\epsilon\,[0, 1]$. It is easy to verify that $\hat{u} < \hat{u}^b$ for all $\alpha\epsilon[0, 1]$. *A pooling equilibrium in which X_1 and X_2 are sold as a bundle with equal amounts of both goods in each bundle is Pareto superior to a pooling equilibrium in which the goods are sold in standalone markets.*

It remains to be shown that in the bundling equilibrium no group of individuals has an incentive, when the goods are also offered separately in stand-alone markets, to choose to purchase them separately. In a bundling equilibrium, all individuals purchase 1 unit of the bundle, $\hat{x}_1^b = 1$. Hence, the type α individual's marginal utility of X_1 is $\hat{u}_1^b = \alpha$. This individual will purchase X_1 separately if and only if $\hat{u}_1^b = \alpha > p_1$.

Suppose that this inequality holds over some interval $\alpha\epsilon[\alpha_0, \alpha_1]$, $0 \le \alpha_0 < \alpha_1 \le 1$, so that individuals in this range purchase X_1 in the stand-alone market. The pooling equilibrium price in this market, p_1, is a *weighted average* of the α's in this range: $\alpha\epsilon[\alpha_0, \alpha_1]$. Hence, for some α this inequality is necessarily violated, contrary to assumption. The same argument applies to X_2.

We conclude that the above bundling equilibrium is "robust", that is, there is no group of individuals who in equilibrium purchase the bundle and also purchase X_1 and X_2 in stand-alone markets.

Typically, there are multiple pooling equilibria. The above example demonstrates that in some equilibria we may find bundling of products, exploiting the negative correlation between the costs of the components of the bundle. We have not explored the general conditions on costs and demands that lead to bundling in equilibrium, leaving this for future analysis.

CHAPTER 16

Financial Innovation—Refundable Annuities (Annuity Options)

16.1 THE TIMING OF ANNUITY PURCHASES

In previous chapters (in particular, chapters 8 and 10) we have seen that in the presence of a competitive annuity market, uncertainty with respect to the length of life can be perfectly insured by an optimum policy that invests all individual savings in long-term annuities. The implication of associating annuity purchases with savings is that the bulk of annuities are purchased throughout one's working life. This stands in stark contrast to empirical evidence that most private annuities are purchased at ages close to retirement (in the United States the average age of annuity purchasers is 62).

A recent survey in the United Kingdom (Gardner and Wadsworth, 2004) reports that half of the individuals in the sample would, given the option, never annuitize. This attitude is independent of specific annuity terms and prices. By far, the dominant reason given for the reluctance to annuitize was a *preference for flexibility*. For those willing to annuitize, the major factors that affected their decisions were health (those in good health were more likely to annuitize), education, household size (less likely to annuitize as household size increases), and income (higher earnings support annuitization).

Lack of flexibility in holding annuities was interpreted by the respondents as the inability to short-sell (or borrow against) early purchased annuities when personal circumstances make such a sale desirable. A preference for selling annuities arises typically upon the realization of negative information about longevity (disability) or income. In this survey, the reluctance to purchase annuities early in life was hardly affected by the knowledge that annuities purchased later would be more expensive (due to adverse selection).

Bodie (2003) also attributes the reluctance to annuitize to uncertain needs for long-term care: "Retired people do not voluntarily annuitize much of their wealth. One reason may be that they believe they need to hold on to assets in case they need nursing home care. Annuities, once bought, tend to be illiquid..."

Data about the timing of annuity purchases and surveys such as the above suggest a need to develop a model that incorporates uninsurable risks, such as income (or needs such as long-term care) in addition to longevity risk. Further, to respond to the desire of individuals for flexibility, the model should allow for short sales of annuities purchased early or the purchase of additional short-term annuities when so desired. The first part of this chapter builds on a model developed by Brugiavini (1993) with this objective in mind.

With uncertainty extending to variables other than longevity, competitive annuity markets cannot attain a first-best allocation (which requires income transfers accross states of nature). Sequential annuity market equilibrium is characterized by the purchase of long-term annuities, short sale of some of these annuities later on, or the purchase of additional short-term annuities.

Since the competitive equilibrium is second best, it is natural to ask whether there are financial instruments that, if available, are welfare-improving. We answer this question in the affirmative, proposing a new type of *refundable annuities*. These are annuities that can be refunded, if so desired, at a predetermined price. Holding a portfolio of such refundable annuities with varying refund prices allows individuals more flexibility in adjusting their consumption path upon the arrival later in life of information about longevity and income.

We show that *refundable annuities* are equivalent to *annuity options*. These are options that entitle the holder to purchase annuities at a later date at a predetermined price.

Interestingly, annuity options are available in the United Kingdom. It is worth quoting again from a textbook for actuaries

> *Guaranteed Annuity Options.* The option may not be exercised until a future date ranging perhaps from 5 to 50 years hence.... The mortality and interest assumptions should be conservative.... The estimates of future improvement implied by experience from which mortality tables were constructed suggest that there should be differences in rates according to the year in which the option is exercisable.... A difference of about $\frac{1}{4}$% in the yield per £100 purchase price could arise between one option and another exercisable ten years later.... [Such] differences in guaranteed annuity rates according to the future date on which they are exercisable do therefore seem to be justified in theory. (Fisher and Young, 1965, p. 421.)

Behavioral economics, addressing bounded rationality (see below) seems to provide additional support to the offer of annuity options that involve a small present cost and allow postponement of the decision to purchase annuities. It has been argued (e.g., Thaler and Benartzi, 2004; Laibson, 1997) that these features provide a positive inducement to purchase annuities for individuals with tendencies to procrastinate or heavily discount the short-run future.

16.2 Sequential Annuity Market Equilibrium Under Survival Uncertainty

Individuals live for two or three periods. Their longevity prospects are unknown in period zero. They learn their period 2 survival probability, p ($0 \leq p \leq 1$), at the beginning of period 1. Survival probabilities have a continuous distribution function, $F(p)$, with support $[\underline{p}, \overline{p}] \in [0, 1]$. In period 0, all individuals earn the same income, y_0, and do not consume. They purchase (long-term) annuities, each of which pays 1 in period 2 if the holder of the annuity is alive (all individuals survive to period 1). Denote the amount of these annuities by a_0 and their price by q_0. Individuals can also save in nonannuitized assets which, for simplicity, are assumed to carry a zero rate of interest. The amount of savings in period 0 is $y_0 - q_0 a_0$.

At the beginning of period 1 (the working years), individuals earn an income, y_1, learn about their survival probability, p, $\overline{p} \geq p \geq \underline{p}$, and make decisions about their consumption in period 1, c_1, and in period 2, c_2 (if alive). They may purchase additional one-period (short-term) annuities, a_1, $a_1 \geq 0$, or short-sell an amount b_1 of period-0 annuities, $b_1 \geq 0$. Since some consumption is invaluable, they will never sell *all* their long-term annuities; that is, $a_0 - b_1 > 0$. In period 2, annuities' payout is $a_0 + a_1 - b_1$ if the holder of the annuities is alive, and 0 if the holder is dead.

(a) First Best

Suppose that income in period 1, y_1, is known with certainty so that individuals are distinguished only by their realized survival probabilities in period 1.

Expected lifetime utility, V, is

$$V = E[u(c_1) + pu(c_2)], \tag{16.1}$$

where $u'(c) > 0$, $u''(c) < 0$ and the expectation is over $p \in [\underline{p}, \overline{p}]$.

The economy's resource constraint is

$$E[c_1 + pc_2] = y_0 + y_1. \tag{16.2}$$

Optimum consumption, the solution to maximization of (16.1) subject to (16.2), may depend on p, $(c_1^*(p), c_2^*(p))$. However, the concavity of V

and the linear constraint yield a first-best allocation that is independent of p: $c_1^*(p) = c_2^*(p) = c^*$, where

$$c^* = \frac{y_0 + y_1}{1 + E(p)}, \tag{16.3}$$

and

$$E(p) = \int_{\underline{p}}^{\bar{p}} p\, dF(p) \tag{16.4}$$

is the expected lifetime. We shall now show that a competitive long-term annuity market attains the first-best allocation.

(b) Annuity Market Equilibrium: No Late Transactions

In period 1, the issuers of annuities can distinguish between those who purchase additional annuities (lenders) and those who short-sell period-0 annuities (borrowers). Since borrowing and lending activities are distinguishable, their prices may be different. Denote the lending price by q_1^1 and the borrowing price by q_1^2.

The individual's maximization is solved backward: Given a_0, p, q_1^1, and q_1^2, individuals in period 1 maximize utility,

$$\max_{a_1 \geq 0,\ b_1 \geq 0} [u(c_1) + pu(c_2)], \tag{16.5}$$

where

$$\begin{aligned} c_1 &= y_0 + y_1 - q_0 a_0 - q_1^1 a_1 + q_1^2 b_1, \\ c_2 &= a_0 + a_1 - b_1. \end{aligned} \tag{16.6}$$

The first-order conditions are

$$-u'(c_1)q_1^1 + pu'(c_2) \leq 0 \tag{16.7}$$

and

$$u'(c_1)q_1^2 - pu'(c_2) \leq 0. \tag{16.8}$$

Denote the solutions to (16.6)–(16.8) by $\hat{a}_1(p)$, $\hat{b}_1(p)$, $\hat{c}_1(p)$, and $\hat{c}_2(p)$, where we suppress the dependence on $y_0 - q_0 a_0$, q_1^1, q_1^2, and y_1. It can be shown (see the appendix) that when $\hat{a}_1(p) > 0$, so (16.7) holds with equality, $\partial \hat{a}_1/\partial p > 0$, and that when $\hat{b}_1(p) > 0$, so (16.8) holds with equality, $\partial \hat{b}_1/\partial p < 0$. A higher survival probability increases the amount of lending and decreases the amount of borrowing whenever these are positive.

Assume that optimum consumption is strictly positive, $\hat{c}_i(p) > 0$, $i = 1, 2$, for all $\underline{p} \leq p \leq \bar{p}$ (a sufficient condition is that $u'(0) = \infty$).

When $q_1^2 < q_1^1$, then by (16.7) and (16.8), individuals are either lenders ($\hat{a}_1 > 0$) or borrowers ($\hat{b}_1 > 0$) but not both. It is shown below that this condition always holds in equilibrium.

In period 0, individuals choose an amount a_0 that maximizes expected utility, anticipating optimum behavior in period 1:

$$\max_{a_0 \geq 0} E[u(\hat{c}_1) + pu(\hat{c}_2)] \tag{16.9}$$

subject to (16.6). By the envelope theorem, the first-order condition is

$$-E[u'(\hat{c}_1)]q_0 + E[pu'(\hat{c}_2)] = 0. \tag{16.10}$$

Denote the optimum amount of period 0 annuities by $\hat{a}_0$. Since in period 0 all individuals are alike and purchase the same amount of annuities, the equilibrium price, $\hat{q}_0$, is equal to expected lifetime, (16.4),

$$\hat{q}_0 = E(p). \tag{16.11}$$

The equilibrium prices of a_1 and of b_1 are determined as follows.

When (16.7) holds with equality at the "kink," $\hat{a}_1 = \hat{b}_1 = 0$, this determines a survival probability, p_a, $p_a = \lambda q_1^1$, where

$$\lambda = \frac{u'(y_0 + y_1 - E(p)\hat{a}_0)}{u'(\hat{a}_0)}, \tag{16.12}$$

with $\hat{a}_0$ determined by (16.10) and (16.11):

$$- E[u'(y_0 + y_1 - E(p)\hat{a}_0 - q_1^1\hat{a}_1(p) + q_1^2\hat{b}_1(p))]E(p)$$
$$+ E[pu'(\hat{a}_0 + \hat{a}_1(p) - \hat{b}_1(p))] = 0. \tag{16.13}$$

When $\hat{a}_1(p) = \hat{b}_1(p) = 0$ for all p, $\bar{p} \geq p \geq \underline{p}$, then, from (16.13), $\lambda = 1$ (because marginal utilities are independent of p). When $p_a < \bar{p}$, then, by (16.7), $\hat{a}_1(p) > 0$ for $\bar{p} \geq p \geq p_a$ and $\hat{a}_1(p) = 0$ for $p_a \geq p \geq \underline{p}$.

Using a similar argument for short sales, define $p_b = \lambda q_1^2$. The condition $q_1^2 < q_1^1$ implies that $p_b < p_a$. It can be seen from (16.8) that if $p_b > \underline{p}$, then $\hat{b}_1 > 0$ for $\underline{p} \leq p < p_b$ and $\hat{b}_1 = 0$ for $\bar{p} \geq p \geq p_b$. Summarizing,

$$
\begin{aligned}
\hat{a}_1 > 0, \ \hat{b}_1 = 0, && p_a < p \leq \bar{p}, \\
\hat{a}_1 = \hat{b}_1 = 0, && p_b \leq p \leq p_a, \\
\hat{b}_1 > 0, \ \hat{a}_1 = 0, && \underline{p} \leq p < p_b.
\end{aligned} \tag{16.14}
$$

The equilibrium prices $\hat{q}_1^1$ and $\hat{q}_1^2$ are determined by zero expected profits conditions

$$\int_{p_a}^{\overline{p}} (\hat{q}_1^1 - p)\hat{a}_1(p)\, dF(p) = 0 \tag{16.15}$$

and

$$\int_{\underline{p}}^{p_b} (\hat{q}_1^2 - p)\hat{b}_1(p)\, dF(p) = 0. \tag{16.16}$$

Note that the bounds of integration, p_a and p_b, depend on the equilibrium values $\hat{q}_1^1$ and $\hat{q}_1^2$. As shown in chapter 8 and first stated by Brugiavini (1993), equilibrium prices that satisfy (16.15) and (16.16) are $q_1^1 = \overline{p}$ and $q_1^2 = \underline{p}$, which implies that $\hat{a}_1 = \hat{b}_1 = 0$ for all p. Under a certain condition, this solution is unique. Proof is provided in the appendix to this chapter. This solution entails that $\hat{c}_1(p)$ and $\hat{c}_2(p)$ are independent of p and, by (16.13), equal to the first-best allocation, $\hat{c}_i(p) = c^*$, $i = 1, 2$, given by (16.3).

Conclusion: *When uncertainty is confined to future survival probabilities, consumers purchase early in life an amount of annuities that generates zero demand for annuities in older ages, ensuring a consumption path that is independent of the state of nature ($\hat{c}_1$ and $\hat{c}_2$ independent of p). Consequently, there will be no annuity transactions late in life.*

This conclusion is in stark contrast to overwhelming empirical evidence showing that private annuities are purchased by individuals at advanced ages.[1] Indeed, we shall now show that the above conclusion does not carry over to more realistic cases with uncertainty about (uninsurable) future variables, such as income, in addition to survival probabilities.

16.3 Uncertain Future Incomes: Existence of a Separating Equilibrium

Suppose that in period 0, the probability of survival to period 2 *and* the level of income in period 1, y_1, are both uncertain, the realizations occurring at the beginning of period 1.[2] The realized levels of p and y_1

---

[1] See Brown et al. (2001).

[2] An alternative formulation is to make utility in period 1 depend on a parameter *needs*, whose value is unknown in period 0 and realized at the beginning of period 1. This formulation yields the same results as those shown below.

are assumed to be private information unknown to the issuers of annuities. For simplicity, assume that y_1 is distributed independently of p. Its distribution, denoted by $G(y_1)$, has a support $(\underline{y}_1, \bar{y}_1)$.

(a) First Best

As before, the first-best allocation maximizes expected utility, (16.1), subject to the resource constraint

$$E\left[c_1 + pc_2\right] = y_0 + E(y_1).$$

Again, the solution is independent of p:

$$c_1^* = c_2^* = \frac{y_0 + E(y_1)}{1 + E(p)}. \tag{16.17}$$

However, unlike the previous case where the early purchase of annuities could fully insure against survival uncertainty and, consequently, implement the first-best allocation, it is seen from (16.17) that the first-best solution with income uncertainty requires income transfers, providing the expected level of income to everyone. Indeed, income insurance would enable such transfers. However, for obvious reasons, the level of realized income is assumed to be private information, and this precludes insurance contingent on the level of income. Consequently, the annuity market cannot, in general, attain the first-best allocation.

(b) Sequential Annuity Market Equilibrium

As before, maximization is done backward. In period 1, utility maximization with respect to a_1 yields the first-order condition

$$-u_1'(\hat{c}_1)q_1^1 + pu'(\hat{c}_2) \leq 0, \tag{16.18}$$

with equality when $\hat{a}_1 > 0$. Setting $\hat{a}_1 = \hat{b}_1 = 0$, (16.18), with equality

$$-u'(y_0 - q_0 a_0 + \tilde{y}_1^1(p)) q_1^1 + pu'(a_0) = 0, \tag{16.19}$$

defines for each p a critical level of income, $\tilde{y}_1^1(p)$. Since $-u'(y_0 - q_0 a_0 + y_1 + q_1^2 b_1)q_1^1 + pu'(a_0 - b_1) > 0$ for all $y_1 > \tilde{y}_1^1(p)$ and $b_1 \geq 0$, it follows that $\hat{a}_1(p, y_1) > 0$ for all $\bar{y}_1 \geq y_1 > \tilde{y}_1^1(p)$ and $\hat{a}_1(p, y_1) = 0$ for all $\underline{y}_1 \leq y_1 < \tilde{y}_1^1(p)$ (see figure 16.1).

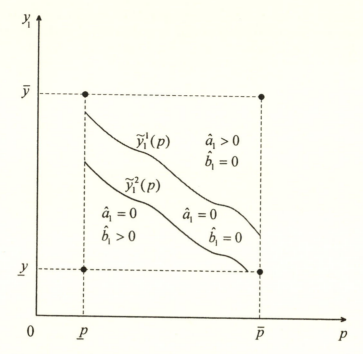

Figure 16.1. Pattern of period-1 annuity purchases.

Similarly, the first-order condition with respect to b_1 is

$$u'(\hat{c}_1)q_1^2 - pu'(\hat{c}_2) \leq 0, \qquad (16.20)$$

with equality when $\hat{b}_1 > 0$. Again, setting $\hat{a}_1 = \hat{b}_1 = 0$, (16.20) with equality defines for each p a critical level of income, $\tilde{y}_1^2(p)$. Since $u'(y_0 - q_0a_0 + y_1)q_1^2 - pu'(a_0) > 0$ for all $\underline{y}_1 \leq y_1 < \tilde{y}_1^2(p)$ and $\hat{a}_1 \geq 0$, it follows that $\hat{b}_1(p, y_1) > 0$ for all $\underline{y}_1 \leq y_1 < \tilde{y}_1^2(p)$ and $\hat{b}_1(p, y_1) = 0$ for all $\bar{y}_1 \geq y_1 > \tilde{y}_1^2(p)$.

To make the pattern displayed in figure (16.1) consistent, it is necessary that $\tilde{y}_1^2(p) < \tilde{y}_1^1(p)$ for all p, which is equivalent to the condition that $q_1^2 < q_1^1$. That is, the borrowing price is lower than the lending price.[3] We shall show that this condition is always satisfied in equilibrium.

[3] For a 2×2 case, Brugiavini (1993) shows that the condition is that income variability be large relative to the variability of survival probabilities. This ensures that all individuals with a high income and with any survival probability purchase annuities, and vice versa.

Equilibrium prices, $(\hat{q}_1^1, \hat{q}_1^2)$, are defined by zero expected profits conditions

$$\int_{\underline{p}}^{\bar{p}} (\hat{q}_1^1 - p)\hat{a}_1(p, \cdot) \, dF(p) = 0 \qquad (16.21)$$

and

$$\int_{\underline{p}}^{\bar{p}} (\hat{q}_1^2 - p)\hat{b}_1(p, \cdot) \, dF(p) = 0, \qquad (16.22)$$

where $\hat{a}_1(p, \cdot) = \int_{\tilde{y}_1^1(p)}^{\bar{y}_1} \hat{a}_1(p, y_1) \, dG(y_1)$ and $\hat{b}_1(p, \cdot) = \int_{\underline{y}_1}^{\tilde{y}_1^2(p)} \hat{b}_1(p, y_1) \, dG(y_1)$ are total demands for a_1 and b_1, respectively, by all relevant income recipients with a given p.

Recall that $\hat{a}_1$ and $\hat{b}_1$ depend implicitly on q_1^1 and q_1^2 and on $\tilde{y}_1^1(p)$ and $\tilde{y}_1^2(p)$, defined above. Thus, the existence and uniqueness of $(\hat{q}_1^1, \hat{q}_1^2)$, defined by (16.20) and (16.21), requires certain conditions.

From (16.21) and (16.22),

$$\hat{q}_1^1 - \hat{q}_1^2 = \int_{\underline{p}}^{\bar{p}} p\varphi(p) \, dF(p), \qquad (16.23)$$

where

$$\varphi(p) = \frac{\hat{a}_1(p, \cdot)}{\int_{\underline{p}}^{\bar{p}} \hat{a}_1(p, \cdot) \, dF(p)} - \frac{\hat{b}_1(p, \cdot)}{\int_{\underline{p}}^{\bar{p}} \hat{b}_1(p, \cdot) \, dF(p)}. \qquad (16.24)$$

Clearly, $\int_{\underline{p}}^{\bar{p}} \varphi(p) \, dF(p) = 0$. Hence, $\varphi(p)$ changes sign at least once over $[\underline{p}, \bar{p}]$. Since $\hat{a}_1(p, \cdot)$ strictly increases and $\hat{b}_1(p, \cdot)$ strictly decreases in p, $\varphi(p)$ strictly increases in p. This implies that there exists a unique $\tilde{p}$, $0 < \tilde{p} < 1$, such that $\varphi(p) \lesseqgtr 0$ as $p \lesseqgtr \tilde{p}$. It follows that

$$\hat{q}_1^1 - \hat{q}_1^2 = \int_{\underline{p}}^{\bar{p}} p\varphi(p) \, dF(p) > \tilde{p} \int_{\underline{p}}^{\bar{p}} \varphi(p) \, dF(p) = 0. \qquad (16.25)$$

Thus, the condition for an equilibrium with active lending and borrowing in period 1 is satisfied.

As before, the equilibrium price for period-0 annuities is equal to life expectancy:

$$\hat{q}_0 = E(p) = \int_{\underline{p}}^{\bar{p}} p \, dF(p). \qquad (16.26)$$

Of course, $0 < \hat{q}_0 < 1$. Notice that since $\hat{a}_1(p, \cdot)$ strictly increases and $\hat{b}_1(p, \cdot)$ strictly decreases in p, $1 > \hat{q}_1^1 > \hat{q}_0$, while $\hat{q}_1^2 < \hat{q}_0$, reflecting the adverse selection in period 1.

We have established that with uncertainties other than longevity there is an active market for annuities late in life, which is consistent with observed patterns of private annuity purchases.

16.4 Refundable Annuities

When uncertainty early in life is confined to longevity then, the optimum purchase of long-term annuities provides perfect protection against this uncertainty. Consequently, all annuity transactions occur early in life with no residual activities at later ages and hence no *adverse selection* occurs. In contrast, when faced with uninsurable uncertainties in addition to longevity, individuals are induced to adjust their portfolios upon the arrival of new information. These adjustments are characterized by adverse selection, reflected in a higher price for (short-term) annuities purchased and a lower price for annuities sold. Recall that in the above discussion we allowed the purchase of short-term annuities late in life as well as the short sale of long-term annuities purchased earlier. In spite of these "pro-market" assumptions, asymmetric information generates adverse selection.

In these circumstances, the following question emerges: Are there financial instruments which, if available, may improve the market allocation in terms of expected utility?[4] We answer this question in the affirmative by proposing a new financial instrument that may achieve this goal. The proposal is to have *a new class of annuities, each carrying a guaranteed commitment by the issuer to refund the annuity, when presented by the holder, at a (pre) specified price. Call these (guaranteed) refundable annuities.*

As shown below, the short sale of annuities purchased in period 0 is equivalent to the purchase in period 0 of refundable annuities whose refund price is equal to $\hat{q}_1^2$. Therefore, in order to improve upon this allocation, it is proposed that individuals hold a portfolio composed of *a variety of refundable annuities with different refund prices*. The purchase of refundable annuities with different refund prices will provide more flexibility in adjusting consumption to the arrival of information about longevity and income. With regular annuities, the revenue *per annuity* from short sales in period 1 is independent of the quantity of annuities sold. With a variety of refundable annuities, this revenue may vary: depending on the realization of longevity and income, individuals will sell refundable annuities in *descending order,* from the highest guaranteed refund price down.

---

[4] We mean instruments that work via individual incentives, in contrast to fiscal means, such as taxes/subsidies, available to the government.

A portfolio of refundable annuities with different refund prices will enable these adjustments to be more closely related to realization of the level of income and longevity and provide more flexibility to individuals' decisions about their optimum consumption paths.

Formally, within the context of the previous three-period model, the market for refundable annuities works as follows. Define a *refundable annuity of type r* as an annuity purchased in period 0 with a guaranteed refund price of $r \geq 0$. This may include annuities with no refund price ($r = 0$). As before, individuals may borrow against these annuities at the market price for borrowing, described in the previous section. Denote the amount of type r annuities by a_0^r, $a_0^r \geq 0$, and the amount refunded by b_1^r, $a_0^r \geq b_1^r \geq 0$.

Consider first only one type of refundable annuity. For any realization of y_1, consumption in periods 1 and 2 is

$$c_1 = y_0 + y_1 - q_0^r a_0^r + r b_1^r - q_1 a_1,$$

$$c_2 = a_0^r - b_1^r + a_1, \tag{16.27}$$

where $a_1 \geq 0$ are (short-term) annuities purchased in period 1 at a price of q_1 and q_0^r is the price of the refundable annuity.[5]

In view of (16.11), maximization of (16.1) with respect to b_1^r and a_1 yields first-order conditions

$$u'(c_1)r - pu'(c_2) \leq 0 \tag{16.28}$$

and

$$-u'(c_1)q_1 + pu'(c_2) \leq 0. \tag{16.29}$$

Denote the solutions to these equations by $\hat{b}_1^r(p, y_1)$, and $\hat{a}_1(p, y_1)$. Again, these functions implicitly depend on $y_0 - q_0^r a_0^r$, r, and q_1. The optimum level of period-0 annuities is determined by maximization of expected utility, (16.3), assuming an optimum choice, $(\hat{c}_1, \hat{c}_2)$, in period 1. The first-order condition is

$$-E[u'(\hat{c}_1)]q_0^r + E[pu'(\hat{c}_2)] = 0. \tag{16.30}$$

---

[5] In period 0 we allow annuities with no refund price ($r = 0$) and individuals may short-sell these annuities in period 1 (borrow) at a market-determined price. For simplicity, we disregard this possibility here. See the appendix.

Extension of the model beyond three periods would allow us to have refundable annuities that can be exercised at different dates.

Denote the solution to (16.16) by $\hat{a}_0^r$. The equilibrium price, $\hat{q}_0^r$, satisfies a zero expected profits condition:

$$\hat{q}_0^r \hat{a}_0^r = \int_{\underline{p}}^{\bar{p}} p(\hat{a}_0^r - \hat{b}_1^r(p; \cdot)\,dF(p) + r\int_{\underline{p}}^{\bar{p}} \hat{b}_1^r(p; \cdot)\,dF(p)$$

or

$$\hat{q}_0^r = E(p) + \frac{1}{\hat{a}_0^r}\int_{\underline{p}}^{\bar{p}}(r - p)\hat{b}_1^r(p; \cdot)\,dF(p), \qquad (16.31)$$

while $\hat{q}_1$ is determined by (16.8).

Two observations are in place. First, a condition for an active annuity market in period 0 is that $r < \hat{q}_1$. This is equivalent to the requirement above (with no refundable annuities) that $\hat{q}_1^2 < \hat{q}_1^1$. When the refund price exceeds the price of period-1 annuities, $r > \hat{q}_1$, individuals refund all the annuities purchased in period 0, $\hat{b}_1^r(p, y_1) = \hat{a}_0^r$, for all p and y_1. But then, by (16.15), $\hat{q}_0^r = r > \hat{q}_1$. However, when the price of annuities in period 1 is lower than their price in period 0, no annuities are purchased in period 0, $\hat{a}_0^r = 0$.

Second, comparing (16.21) and (16.27), it is seen that *refundable annuities and short sales of period-0 annuities (borrowing) are equivalent when the refund and the borrowing price are equal: $r = \hat{q}_1^2$*. Thus, when short sales is permitted, refundable annuities may be (ex ante) welfare-enhancing if they provide a refund price or a variety of refund prices different from the borrowing equilibrium price.

16.5 A Portfolio of Refundable Annuities

Now suppose that individuals can purchase in period 0 a variety of refundable annuities. Type $r_i \geq 0$ annuities are annuities that each guarantee a refund of r_i when presented by the holder in period 1. There are k types of such refundable annuities, ranked from the highest refund down, $r_1 > r_2 > \cdots > r_k \geq 0$. Denote the price and the amount of type r_i annuities purchased by q_0^i and a_0^i, respectively. The amount of type r_i annuities refunded in period 1 is denoted b_1^i, $a_0^i \geq b_1^i \geq 0$.

Individuals' consumption is now given by

$$c_1 = y_0 + y_1 - \sum_{i=1}^{k} q_0^i a_0^i - q_1 a_1 + \sum_{i=1}^{k} r_i b_1^i \qquad (16.32)$$

and

$$c_2 = \sum_{i=1}^{k}(a_0^i - b_1^i) + a_1. \qquad (16.33)$$

Maximization of (16.5) with respect to a_1 and b_1^i, $i = 1, 2, \ldots, k$, yields first-order conditions

$$-u'(c_1)q_1 + pu'(c_2) \leq 0 \qquad (16.34)$$

and

$$u'(c_1)r_i - pu'(c_2) \leq 0, \quad i = 1, 2, \ldots, k, \qquad (16.35)$$

with equality when $a_1 > 0$ and $b_1^i > 0$, respectively. Denote the solutions to (16.34) and (16.35) by $\hat{a}_1$ and $\hat{b}_1^i$, $i = 1, 2, \ldots, k$. These are functions of $\underline{r} = (r_1, r_2, \ldots, r_k)$, $\bar{q}_0 = (q_0^1, q_0^2, \ldots, q_0^k)$, and q_1.

It is seen from (16.35) that if $\hat{b}_1^i > 0$, then $\hat{b}_1^i = a_0^i$ for all $1 \geq i > j$. That is, *all higher-ranked annuities (compared to marginally refunded annuities) are fully refunded.*

The amount of type r_i annuities purchased in period 0 is determined by maximization of expected utility, (16.9), yielding the first-order condition

$$-E[u'(c_1)]q_0^i + E[pu'(c_2)] \qquad i = 1, 2, \ldots, k, \qquad (16.36)$$

where the expectation is over p and y_1.

The value of holding a diversified optimum portfolio of refundable annuities clearly depends on specific assumptions about risk attitudes (utility function) and the joint distribution of longevity and income. To provide insight plan to do detailed calculations and report them in a separate paper.[6]

16.6 EQUIVALENCE OF REFUNDABLE ANNUITIES AND ANNUITY OPTIONS

We shall now demonstrate that refundable annuities are equivalent to *options to purchase annuities at a later date for a predetermined price.* In terms of the above three-period model, suppose that in period 0 individuals can purchase options, each of which entitles the owner to purchase in period 1 an annuity at a given price. As before, the payout of each annuity is $1 in period 2 if the owner is alive and nothing if they are dead. Denote by $o(\pi)$ the price of an option that, if exercised, entitles the holder to purchase an annuity in period 1 at a price of π. On a time

---

[6] This work involves joint research with Jerry Green of Harvard University, who was instrumental in developing the ideas presented in this chapter.

scale, the scheme showing the equivalence of refundable annuities and annuity options is as follows:

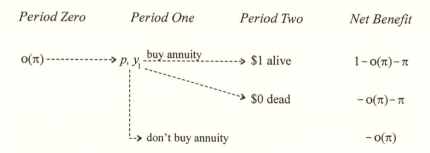

The comparable scheme for refundable annuities is

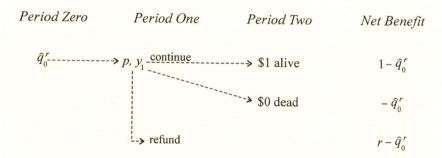

It is seen that for $\hat{q}_0^r = o(\pi) + \pi$ and $r = \pi$ (hence, $o(\pi) = \hat{q}_0^r - r$), these two schemes are equivalent.

In addition to the above discussion about the advantages of the flexibility offered by holding a portfolio of options to annuitize, there may be additional behavioral reasons in favor of such options. A vast economic literature reports experimental and empirical evidence of the bounded rationality and shortsightedness of individuals (e.g., Rabin, 1998, 1999; Mitchell and Utkus, 2004). Of particular relevance to our case seems to be the plan designed by Thaler and Benartzi (2004), where individuals commit to save for pensions a certain fraction of future *increases in earnings*. The raison d'etre for this plan is, presumably, the presence of cognitive shortcomings or self-control problems (procrastination, shortsightedness). Individuals are more willing to commit to the purchase of annuities from increases in earnings compared to the purchase by rational individuals. By deliberately delaying implementation of the purchase of annuities, this plan may accommodate *hyperbolic discounters* (Laibson,

1997) who put a high discount rate on short-run saving. Thaler and Benartzi report that their plan has been successfully implemented by a number of firms. There seem to be parallels between the psychological insight that motivated this plan and the proposed annuity options.

Appendix

We have seen in the text that $\hat{b}_1(p) = 0$ when $\hat{a}_1(p) > 0$ and (16.7) holds with equality. Differentiating with respect to p,

$$\frac{\partial \hat{a}_1}{\partial p} = -\frac{1}{p} \left(\frac{1}{\dfrac{u''(\hat{c}_1)}{u'(\hat{c}_1)} q_1^1 + \dfrac{u''(\hat{c}_2)}{u'(\hat{c}_2)}} \right) > 0. \tag{16A.1}$$

Similarly, when $\hat{b}_1(p) > 0$, then $\hat{a}_1(p) = 0$ and (16.8) holds with equality. Differentiating with respect to p,

$$\frac{\partial \hat{b}_1}{\partial p} = \frac{1}{p} \left(\frac{1}{\dfrac{u''(\hat{c}_1)}{u'(\hat{c}_1)} q_1^2 + \dfrac{u''(\hat{c}_2)}{u'(\hat{c}_2)}} \right) < 0. \tag{16A.2}$$

Consider the zero expected profits condition (16.5):

$$\int_{p_a}^{\bar{p}} (q_1^1 - p)\hat{a}_1(p)dF(p) = 0. \tag{16A.3}$$

Where $p_a = \lambda q_1^1$, λ is given by (16.12),

$$\lambda = \frac{u'(y_0 + y_1 - E(p)\hat{a}_0)}{u'(\hat{a}_0)}, \tag{16A.4}$$

and $\hat{a}_0$ is determined by (16.13),

$$-E\left[u'(y_0 + y_1 - E(p)\hat{a}_0 - q_1^1\hat{a}_1(p) + q_1^2\hat{b}_1(p))E(p)\right.$$

$$+E\left[pu'(\hat{a}_0 + \hat{a}_1(p) - \hat{b}_1(p))\right] = 0. \tag{16A.5}$$

When $\hat{a}_1(p) = \hat{b}_1(p) = 0$ for $\bar{p} \geq p \geq \underline{p}$, then $\lambda = 1$ (because in (16A.5), marginal utilities are independent of p). Whenever $\hat{a}_1(p) > 0$ or $\hat{b}_1(p) > 0$ for some ranges of p, this changes $\hat{a}_0$, and hence λ, compared to the previous case.

Denote by φ expected profits in the period-1 market for annuities,

$$\varphi(q_1^1) = \int_{p_a}^{\bar{p}} (q_1^1 - p)\hat{a}_1(p)\,dF(p). \tag{16A.6}$$

An equilibrium price, $\hat{q}_1^1$, is defined by $\varphi(\hat{q}_1^1) = 0$. Since $p_a = \bar{p}$ when $q_1^1 = \bar{p}$ (because $\hat{a}_1(p) = 0$ and $\lambda = 1$), $\hat{q}_1^1 = \bar{p}$ is an equilibrium price, implying no purchase of annuities in period 1. A similar argument applies to the market for b_1: Here the equilibrium price is $\hat{q}_1^2 = \underline{p}$, implying $\hat{b}_1(p) = 0$ for all p.

Could there be another equilibrium with $p_a < \bar{p}$ (and $p_b > \underline{p}$)? Under a "mild" condition the answer is negative.

Suppose that $q_1^1 = E(p)$. Then, by (16.7) and (16.8) and (16A.5), $\hat{a}_0 = 0$ and $\hat{b}_1(p) = 0$ for all $\underline{p} \le p \le \bar{p}$. This is reasonable: When prices of annuities in period 0 and in period 1 are equal, annuities are purchased only in period 1. Then, by (16A.4), $\lambda = 0$. It now follows from (16A.1) and (16A.6) that $\varphi(E(p)) < 0$. A sufficient condition that $\hat{q}_1^1 = \bar{p}$ be the only equilibrium price is that $\varphi(q_1^1)$ strictly increases for all q_1^1, $E(p) < q_1^1 < \bar{p}$. From (16A.6), the condition is

$$\varphi'(q_1^1) = \int_{p_a}^{\bar{p}} \left[\hat{a}_1(p) + (\hat{q}_1^1 - p)\frac{d\hat{a}_1(p)}{dq_1^1} \right] dF(p) > 0. \tag{16A.7}$$

Note that $d\hat{a}_1(p)/dq_1^1$ in (16A.7) is the total derivative of $\hat{a}_1(p)$ with respect to q_1^1, taking into account the equilibrium change in $\hat{a}_0$ (from (16A.5)). Condition (16A.7) ensures that $\varphi(q_1^1) < 0$ for $E(p) \le p < \bar{p}$.

References

Ahn, H., and C. Manski. 1993. Distribution theory for the analysis of binary choice under uncertainty with nonparametric estimation of expectations. *Journal of Econometrics* 56: 291–321.

Angeletos, G., D. Laibson, A. Repetto, J. Tobacman, and S. Weinberg. 2001. The hyperbolic consumption model: Calibration, simulation, and empirical evaluation. *Journal of Economic Perspectives* 15: 47–68.

Arrow, K. 1992. Sex differentiation in annuities: Reactions on utilitarianism and inequality. *Rational Interactions*, R. Selten (ed.). New York: Springer, pp. 333–336.

Atkinson, A., and J. Stiglitz. 1980. *Lectures on Public Economics*. New York: McGraw-Hill.

Austen, J. 1811. *Sense and Sensibility*. New York: Random House.

Baldwin, B. G. 2002. *The New Life Insurance Investment Advisor*, 2nd ed. New York: McGraw-Hill.

Bell, F., and M. Miller. 2005. Life tables for the United States social security area, 1900–2100. *Social Security Actuarial Study* 120, August.

Benartzi, S., and R. H. Thaler. 2004. Save more tomorrow: Using behavioral economics to increase employee saving. *Journal of Political Economy* 112: S164–S187.

Bernheim, D. B., J. Skinner, and S. Weinberg. 2001. What accounts for the variation in retirement wealth among U.S. households? *American Economic Review* 91(4): 832–857.

Biggs, J. H. 1969. Alternatives in variable annuity benefit designs. *Transactions of the Society of Actuaries, Part I* 21(61): 495–517.

Bodie, Z. 2003. Thoughts on the future: Life-cycle investing in theory and practice. *Financial Analysts Journal* January/February: 24–29.

Bowers, N. L., H. U. Gerber, J. C. Hickman, D. A. Jones, and C. J. Nesbitt. 1997. *Actuarial Mathematics*, 2nd ed. Schaumberg, IL: Society of Actuaries.

Brown, J. R., O. S. Mitchell, J. M. Poterba, and M. J. Warshawsky. 2001. *The Role of Annuity Markets in Financing Retirements*. Cambridge, MA: MIT Press.

Brown, J. R., and J. M. Poterba. 2000. Joint life annuities and annuity demand by married couples. *Journal of Risk and Insurance* 67(4): 527–553.

Brugiavini, A. 1993. Uncertainty resolution and the timing of annuity purchases. *Journal of Public Economics* 50: 31–62.

Cannon, E., and I. Tonks. 2002. Annuity prices, money's worth and replacement ratios: U.K. experience, 1972–2002. Bristol, U.K.: CMPO, Working Paper 02/051, September.

Cannon, E., and I. Tonks. 2006. Survey of annuity pricing. Norwich, U.K.: Department for Work and Pensions, Research Report 318.

Chiappori, A., and B. Salanie. 2000. Testing for asymmetric information in insurance markets. *Journal of Political Economy* 108(1): 56–78.

Choi, J., D. Laibson, B. Madrian, and A. Metrick. 2005. Passive decisions and potent defaults. In *Analyses in the Economics of Aging*, D. Wise (ed.). Chicago: University of Chicago Press, pp. 59–78.

Choi, J., D. Laibson, B. Madrian, and A. Metrick. 2006. Saving for retirement on the path of least resistance. In *Behavioral Public Finance*, E. McCaffrey and J. Slemrod (eds.). New York: Russell Sage Foundation, pp. 304–351.

Coale, A. J. 1972. *The Growth and Structure of Human Populations: A Mathematical Investigation*. Princeton: Princeton University Press.

Cutler, D. M. 2004. Are the benefits of medicine worth what we pay for it? Paper presented at the annual Herbert Lourie Memorial Lecture on Health Policy, Syracuse, NY.

Cutler, D. M., A. S. Deaton, and A. Lleras-Muney. 2006. The determinants of mortality. Cambridge, MA: National Bureau of Economic Research, Working Paper 11963, January.

Davidoff, T., J. R. Brown, and P. A. Diamond. 2005. Annuities and individual welfare. *American Economic Review* 95(5):1573–1590.

Deaton, A., and C. Paxson (1997). The effects of economic and population growth on national savings and inequality, *Demography* 34: 97–114.

Diamond, P. A. 2003. *Taxation, Incomplete Markets and Social Security*. Cambridge, MA: MIT Press.

Diamond, P. 1977. A framework for social security analysis. *Journal of Public Economics* 8: 275–298.

Diamond, P., and B. Köszegi. 2003. Quasi-hyperbolic discounting and retirement. *Journal of Public Economics* 87: 1839–1872.

Diamond, P. A., and J. A. Mirrlees. 1971. Optimal taxation and public production. I: Production efficiency and II: Tax Rules. *American Economic Review* 61(1): 8–27 and 261–278.

Duncan, R. M. 1952. A retirement system granting unit annuities and investing in equities. *Transaction of the Society of Actuaries* 4(9): 317–344.

Finkelstein, A., and J. Poterba. 2002. Selection effects in the United Kingdom individual annuities market. *Economic Journal* 112: 28–50.

Finkelstein, A., and J. Poterba. 2004. The adverse selection in insurance markets: Policyholder evidence from the U.K. annuity market. *Journal of Political Economy* 112(1): 183–208.

Fisher, H. F., and J. Young. 1965. Actuarial Practice of Life Assurance: A Textbook for Actuarial students. New York: Cambridge University Press.

Gan, L., M. Hurd, and D. McFadden. 2003. Individual subjective survival curves. Cambridge, MA: National Bureau of Economic Research, Working Paper 9480, January.

Gardner, J., and M. Wadsworth. 2004. Who would buy an annuity? An empirical investigation. Watson Wyatt Technical Paper Series, Working Paper 12, March.

Gerber, H. 1990. *Life Insurance Mathematics*. New York: Springer.

Harris, C., and D. Laibson. 2001. Dynamic choices of hyperbolic consumers. *Econometrica* 69: 935–957.

http://en.wikipedia.org/wiki/Annuity_%28 US_financial_products%29

Hurd, M. D., D. McFadden, and A. Merrill. 1999. Predictors of mortality among the elderly. Cambridge, MA: National Bureau of Economic Research, Working Paper 7440, December.

Hurd, M., and K. McGarry. 1993. Evaluation of subjective probability distributions in the HRS. Cambridge, MA: National Bureau of Economic Research, Working Paper 4560, December.

Hurd, M. D., J. P. Smith, and J. M. Zissimopoulos. 2002. The effects of subjective survival on retirement and social security claiming. Cambridge, MA: National Bureau of Economic Research, Working Paper 9140, September.

Hurd, M. D., and S. Rohwedder. 2006. Some answers to the retirement – consumption puzzle. Cambridge, MA: National Bureau of Economic Research, Working Paper 12057, February.

James, E., and X. Song. 2001. Annuities markets around the world: Money's worth and risk intermediation. Center for Research on Pensions and Welfare Policies, Working Paper 16/01.

Jennings, R. M., and A. P. Trout. 1982. *The Tontine: From the Reign of Louis XIV to the French Revolutionary Era,* Huebner Foundation Monograph No. 12. Philadelphia: The Wharton School, University of Pennsylvania.

Kinugasa, T., and A. Mason. 2007. Why countries become wealthy: The effects of adult longevity on savings. *World Development,* 35, 1–23.

Kotlikoff, L. J., and A. Spivak. 1981. The family as an incomplete annuities market. *Journal of Political Economy* 89(2): 372–391.

Kopczuk, W., and J. Lupton. 2007. To leave or not to leave: The distribution of bequest motives, National Bureau of Economic Research, Working Paper No. 11767.

Kotlikoff, L., and L. Summers. 1981. The role of intergenerational transfers in aggregate capital accumulation, *Journal of Political Economy,* 89, 706–732.

Laffont, J. -J., and D. Martimort. 2002. *Theory of Incentives.* Princeton: Princeton University Press.

Laibson, D. 1997. Golden eggs and hyperbolic discounting. *Quarterly Journal of Economics* 62: 443–477.

Laibson, D. 2003. Intertemporal decision making. In *Encyclopedia of Cognitive Science.* London: Nature Publishing Group.

Lee, R., A. Mason, and T. Miller. 2001. Saving, wealth and the demographic transition in East Asia. In *Population Change and Economic Development in East Asia,* A. Mason (ed.). Stanford: Stanford University Press, pp. 155–184.

Levy, H. 1998. *Decision Making Under Uncertainty: Stochastic Dominance.* Boston: Kluwer Academic Publishers.

Miles, D. 1999. Modelling the impact of demographic change upon the Economy, *Economic Journal,* 109: 1–36.

Milevsky, M. A. 2006. The Calculus of Retirement Income: Financial Models for Pension Annuities and Life Insurance. New York: Cambridge University Press.

Mirrlees, J. A. 1971. An exploration in the theory of optimum income taxation. *Review of Economic Studies* 38(2): 175–208.

Murtaugh, M., B. C. Spillman, and M. J. Warshawsky. 2001. In sickness and in health: An annuity approach to financing long-term care and retirement income. *Journal of Risk and Insurance* 68: 225–253.

Myles, G. 1995. *Public Economics*. New York: Cambridge University Press.

Pindyck, R., and D. Rubinfeld. 2000. *Microeconomics*. Upper Saddle River, NJ: Pearson Prentice Hall.

Rabin, M. 1998. Psychology and economics. *Journal of Economic Literature* 36: 11–46.

Ramsey, F. P. 1927. A contribution to the theory of taxation. *Economic Journal* 37(145): 47–61.

Rothschild, M., and J. Stiglitz. 1976. Equilibrium in competitive insurance markets: An essay on the economics of incomplete information. *Quarterly Journal of Economics* 90: 624–649.

Salanie, B. 2000. *Microeconomics of Market Failure*. Cambridge, MA: MIT Press.

Salanie, B. 2003. *The Economics of Taxation*. Cambridge, MA: MIT Press.

Sheshinski, E. 2003. Annuities and retirement. In *Assets, Beliefs, and Equilibria in Economic Dynamics*, D. Aliprantis, K. Arrow, P. Hammond, F. Kubler, H. M. Wu, and N. Yannelis (eds.). New York: Springer, pp. 27–54.

World Bank. 1994. Averting the Old Age Crisis: Policies to Protect the Old and Promote Growth. Oxford: Oxford University Press.

Yaari, M. 1965. Uncertain lifetime, life insurance and the theory of the consumer. *Review of Economic Studies* 32: 137–150.

Index